Spiritual Intimacy:

What You Really Want with a Mate

SONDRA RAY

and

MARKUS RAY

Books By Sondra Ray

Liberation Breathing: The Divine Mother's Gift
Birth and Relationships: How Your Birth Affects Your Relationships
Celebration of Breath
Drinking the Divine
Essays on Creating Sacred Relationships
Healing and Holiness
How to Be Chic, Fabulous and Live Forever
I Deserve Love
Ideal Birth
Inner Communion
Interludes with the Gods
Loving Relationships: The Secrets of a Great Relationship
Loving Relationships II
Pele's Wish: Secrets of the Hawaiian Masters and Eternal Life
Pure Joy
Rebirthing in the New Age
Rock Your World with the Divine Mother
The Loving Relationships Treasury
The Only Diet There Is

Books by Markus Ray

Odes to the Divine Mother
Liberation Breathing: The Divine Mother's Gift

Sondra Ray and Markus Ray Online

Www.sondraray.com publishes the most recent writings and creations by Sondra Ray and Markus Ray and serves as a community resource, providing information on seminars, trainings, private sessions, contacts, and practitioners available to you worldwide. See them on Facebook and Twitter.

PAGE PUBLISHING, INC. New York, NY
in co-operation with
IMMORTAL RAY PRODUCTIONS, Nashville, TN

Immortal Ray Productions
Nashville

First originally published by Page Publishing, Inc. 2015

Page Publishing, Inc.
101 Tyrellan Avenue, Suite 100
New York, NY 10309
www.PagePublishing.com

Immortal Ray Productions
3000 Vanderbilt Place #118
Nashville, TN 37212
www.SondraRay.com, ImmortalRayProductions@gmail.com

First Edition, 2015

ISBN 978-1-68139-931-7 (pbk),
ISBN 978-1-68139-932-4 (digital)

Printed in the United States of America

Cover Photo: Judy Totton of London.
www.judytotton.com

Contents

Preface

After my divorce in the early 1970s, I had a mystical experience where a voice told me to move to California immediately. I left the next day. When I got there, I began to look for a seminar on relationships. There were many seminars popping up, but I could not find one on relationships. So I asked people, "Where can I find a seminar on relationships?" They all said, "Everyone is too screwed up in that area to teach it!" Then I wondered, "Does it have to be me then?" As a matter of fact, I turned out to be one of the first "rebirthers"/"breath-workers" in the world fortunately. My clients would come to me after a few sessions and begin to tell me all their problems about sex, relationships, and marriage. I would give them a rebirthing session, and they would have a memory of their birth, and then I noticed something revolutionary. I was able to see how what happened at their birth was affecting their intimate relationships. It was like light bulbs going off in my head. I was a bit hesitant to talk about it because it seemed way out there. But then one day, the founder of rebirthing, Leonard Orr, came home and said to me, "They want you in Hawaii, and I told them you would come." Wow! Suddenly I was on the road, having never taught a seminar in my life.

I arrived in Hawaii, and there was a group of around twenty-five people sitting on the floor of this house. So I began by saying, "Let me tell what I have learned about how your birth affects your relationships," and I continued to speak as the day went by very quickly. At the end, everyone was just staring at me with their mouths hanging open. They more or less said, "Sondra, this explains everything." I said, "Really?" They then insisted I do the same lecture the next day as they wanted to bring their friends to hear me. The second day, that group had the same experience. They, however, said it was all too powerful to integrate in a one-day experience, and I should write a two-day training. So I went back to San Francisco and began writing the first Loving Relationships Training, the LRT®. I tried it out in a hotel in San Francisco, and one man there was from Hawaii. At the end, he said, "I want to feel like this forever, so I want to move here." I told him that I would be quite willing to do the training in Hawaii if he would organize it. So that is how it all started. It spread very rapidly around the world as breathworkers heard about it through the grapevine and invited me to their cities. My interest in relationships has continued and deepened ever since.

The way I became inspired to have this book title was very interesting to me. Our clients who came to us for Liberation Breathing® (our new expression of rebirthing/breathwork) sessions were complaining that they were bored in their relationships. Their relationships were flat, and they did not have good communication. The more they continued their breathing sessions, the deeper they went spiritually and the more they longed to share their growth and changes with their partners. But they would say things like this:

- "I cannot talk to my mate about this but I would like to."
- "My mate would never go for this kind of work but I want him to."
- "I really miss being able to share these changes with my mate, but he is not interested."
- "My mate supports me in doing this work, but he would never do it."
- "I cannot tell my mate that I am here doing this."
- "I wish I could tell my mate about the changes I am experiencing."
- "We cannot talk about what really matters."

And on and on. You notice this was mostly coming from women.

I started noticing that, especially with the women, they were just craving a deep spiritual connection with their intimate partner. They were craving *spiritual intimacy*. At first it seemed rather hopeless that the men would ever hear what they wanted to share. They were even afraid to try to explain what was happening to them. It also seemed hopeless that the men would come in and get a session themselves. But then I caught myself from thoughts that I was agreeing with their hopelessness instead of offering a higher thought.

I started suggesting ways they could talk to their mate about the work, and I started suggesting that they change the thought that their mate would *never* work on himself. Pretty soon, I started having the men come slowly but surely. Once they came to a session of breathwork and tried it, they liked it also. And so they slowly learned to talk about their own process and spiritual growth. They started getting over being threatened about it. Some of them came and took the New Loving Relationships Training, and then they really opened up. Then they saw the value of staying with the process. We always say that Liberation Breathing® is a lifelong spiritual path. When both persons in the couple commit to it and share about it, they experience a spiritual intimacy they never had before, and it is as if they wake up to a whole new life.

I started to see that was what people really wanted, and it was also true for men although they could not admit it at first. They could not define it like the women could. It was very exciting to see things change over time. If one is really going for enlightenment in this life, one knows one has to work on clearing himself or herself, and this is a lifelong practice. One's spiritual purification must become a top priority. This is not really about religion. It is about being enlightened within. It is about giving up one's false self (ego). It is about being all that one can be. It is about learning to live in bliss.

One of my teachers said there are certain *consciousness factors* which keep us from being in bliss. He listed them as such:

- Birth trauma
- Specific negative thought structures
- Parental disapproval syndrome
- Unconscious death urge
- Other lifetimes
- School trauma
- Religious trauma

Wow, you might say— I never thought I would have to clear all of that! Well the fact is when you do, you get to bliss, and it is actually fun to release all this, and it is such a huge relief!

Even my female spiritual teacher, Ammachi (who is the highest female saint in the physical body at this time), says you have to clear the personal shadow, the family shadow, and the religious shadow. Eventually, these will have to come out, she says. If they come out unconsciously, it really messes up your life. If you consciously release them, then you are *liberated*.

I read somewhere that I should be able to reduce what I do down to three words. I discussed this with my husband Markus and he came up with these three words:

1. Love
2. Liberation
3. Longevity

Wow, I thought he really hit the nail on the head. This book is also about those subjects. Working on those subjects takes your relationship to a whole new level and your enlightenment grows by leaps and bounds.

What I wish for all of you is the *spiritual intimacy* you deserve in your loving relationships. I pray that this book inspires you; and especially that you can put it into practice. If you ever want a Liberation Breathing® session from us directly, contact us. Info is given in the back of this book.

—Sondra Ray !

Introduction

by Markus Ray

Recently, I reviewed a movie by Oliver Stone on The Doors, the rock and roll band from the late 1960s spearheaded by the provocative Jim Morrison. After the fame of The Doors was well entrenched, Morrison began to get fat, his body became very different from the Adonis figure that plummeted him into the pop culture limelight. In a telling scene toward the end of the movie, after all the sex and drugs and rock and roll had taken a physical toll, as shown by the plump waistline of the popular idol, he was challenged by one of his close colleagues about his next move. In light of this fall from Dionysian grace only a short five of six years, what audience would listen to a fat Jimmy? Morrison responded tellingly, like any good poet would.

"You underestimate the audience," he said to Tom Baker, his friend. "You think all they want is two cars and a house? But you are wrong. You really wanna know what they want? *Something sacred.* That's what they want. *Something sacred.*"

On stage, in his shamanistic fashion, that is what Jim Morrison delivered in his break on through to the other side. People don't just want a good career, a Lexus SUV, and a big mansion in the latest gated community suburb. What they really want is *something sacred.* And in their relationship with their mate, that translates into *spiritual intimacy.* They want to feel something transcendent of the day-to-day problems of existence. They want to have an intimacy with their partner, a closeness, which transports them to a wow dimension of *pure joy*. This closeness, which takes them higher to *pure joy*, is *spiritual intimacy*.

Are you experiencing *pure joy* and *spiritual intimacy* in your life and relationships? Most of us have had peak moments of this ecstatic sense of well-being. Most of us have also felt sometimes an underlying discontent or something deeply unsettling in our relationships with life and with our mate. The divorce rate in America is reported at nearly 50 percent. Of the 50 percent of couples who stay together for economic, religious, or moral reasons or who are just too chicken to change, only a fraction of them would deem their relationship in a state of *pure joy*.

Entertainment gives us an outlet to forget about our deep-seated discontent. We listen and watch all kinds of stuff on our iPods and flat-screen TVs and buy our movie tickets on our smart phones. We shop in supermalls for things we may not really need. Running around constantly, we seldom ask in the bigger sense, "Where to?" What is my highest priority in my life and relationship?

Something sacred—where do you find it? What do you need to get it? What can you do to have it in your life and in your relationship permanently? This is what this book by Sondra Ray is about. This is what this book answers. For anyone who is in touch with their deepest desire to know something beyond the acquisition of two cars and a house, something beyond the common family patterns and dynamics of relationships we inherited from our parents and grandparents, this book is for you. It will give you the real picture of where you might be stuck in relationships and the thread out of the labyrinth of your discontent.

Jim Morrison's insight into his audience was astute. Their deepest yearning was for something beyond the material status quo. Their deepest yearning was for a spiritual experience. Even beyond the sex and drugs and rock and roll that motivated the counterculture of the 1960s, there was a more sublime truth that everyone wanted. To know God, something supernatural, and to know God in their relationships with one another, that was what the people wanted then in 1970 and want now in the twenty-first century over forty years later. The yearning and the possibility for a spiritual solution to the happiness factor is still the same, decades after The Doors tragically disbanded after Morrison's untimely death in Paris at age twenty-seven.

A visceral experience of boundlessness was what Morrison sought and found. Yet what could have saved him from the early arms of death evaded his grasp, and perhaps he was compelled by an obsession with a *heavenly* state on the other side. He had achieved fame and fortune, for which he had come to disvalue, and he even attracted an infamous obscenity conviction from the law. But those alone could not have deterred him from life. There was something else missing, and that was the hole in which his death urge got the better of him. "This is the end," was the telling self-prophesy that plummeted him to the underworld never to return.

He had *something sacred* but lacked the *spiritual intimacy* with his life and mate, Pamela Courson, that could have kept him alive and well. Purportedly the drug-induced highs of a heroin addiction got the better of both of them. She died as well of the same fate only a couple years after her consort. *Spiritual intimacy* promises love, liberation, and longevity, something even higher than pop culture notoriety. Sondra Ray puts forth in this book the principles to realize *Spiritual Intimacy: What You Really Want with a Mate*. She does this by showing you the old way of relating that does not work and then the new way that does.

In the old paradigm for relationships, we pretty much did what the cellular memories of our parents and ancestors programmed us to do. We recreated the relationship our parents had, or even searched for the opposite, yet gradually fell back into the familiar patterns that governed our family dynamics we inherited. We marry our parents' relationship, basically, or our opposite reaction to our parents' relationship. We often seek what is familiar even if it is codependent and dysfunctional, leading to depression and malaise. Much of our seeking is ruled by underlying subconscious patterns.

In Sondra Ray's Loving Relationship Training (LRT®), which she has taught around the world since 1974, the common negative family patterns that sabotage relationships are aired and discussed. These patterns are blocks to having true *spiritual intimacy*, therefore, need to be examined and released for real liberation from the past to take place. She describes the fourteen most common repetitive neurotic behaviors that we inherited from our family. We tend to reproduce these in our new relationships (most often unconsciously) and merely repeat the family mistakes of the past in the present. These form the perennial patterns of the old paradigm of relationships that can hardly lead to the peace, joy, and freedom of Eden. Rather, these plunge our marriages and partnerships into a kind of polite hell that we too often tolerate; at worst, fight about; and at best, arrive at mutual resignation, but seldom, within the premises of our family's past, fully overcome.

And we find out in this book, from Sondra's many years as a life teacher and as a practitioner of rebirthing/breathwork, how your actual birth script—your conception, your gestation, your birth, and your postpartum life—affects your relationships. The preverbal thoughts you formed about the world and life, based on this too often traumatic script, highly affect how you relate to people, yourself, your mate and the world. Some of the most common birth scripts are discussed, shedding light on the dynamics of how they may affect your relationships in its uncanny tendency to replay the past.

Probably one of the most insidious saboteurs of life and relationships is what we term in this book and others on the subject of breathwork, the "personal lie." It is the most negative subconscious thought you have about yourself, often formed pre-verbally back to your birth as well. This negative subconsciousness factor often plays havoc on relationships. Everyone has one unless you are fully enlightened like Babaji, Jesus, or Ammachi. And we like to say, until you are like Jesus performing miracles on your own, you have something to clear. *Spiritual intimacy* helps you locate, clear, forgive, and release your *personal lie* and encourages regular practices like meditation, following the principles in the book *A Course in Miracles*, and Liberation Breathing® to breathe it out of your very cells, so you will not remain a victim of this thought.

Sondra cites the *personal lie* of a public figure we all know to demonstrate the havoc reeking tendency of this negative subconscious thought. Michael Jackson's *personal lie* was obviously, "I am bad." He made a bloody fortune singing that song then he became bad with all the child molestation accusations and then he kicked the bucket in the mental quagmire of a drug-induced death, never having liberated himself from that thought. We tend to avoid seeing the shadows we live under. This avoidance is killing us basically. *Spiritual intimacy* can observe the shadows, forgive them, and let them go. But if one does not shine a forgiving light upon these shadows, they will continue to perpetuate their negative effects.

It is obvious that anger and conflict destroy relationships. But the fact is anger is never really justified (*A Course in Miracles*, T30 VI, 1–1). This is often hard for people to get. We are so accustomed to justifying our reasons for being angry that we do not stop and see anger's self-destructive nature. *Spiritual intimacy* is the solution to anger, the choice for peace above all else. This book gives you a practical process to drop your anger and move on. It encourages you to study *A Course in Miracles*, which says, "Forgiveness is the key to happiness" and the escape from anger (*A Course,* WB lesson 121). The *forgiveness diet* that Sondra Ray introduced in earlier books is mentioned again and is still the best solution in present time to liberate yourself from anger completely.

There are two parts to this book. Part 1 examines the old paradigm of what does not work in relationships and why. Part 2 gives you a new foundation to build relationships based on *spiritual intimacy* and self-awareness. Both parts suggest a new mind is needed to put you in a higher frequency of thought you have perhaps never experienced before. In this new mind, the "new frequency" for relationships makes a measure of music in the harmonies of love, liberation, and longevity. Love is the vibration of no conflict. It is one of peace and joy. Liberation from negative thoughts and cellular memory is now your top priority, and you become more receptive to attract the right mate or transform through love an existing relationship. Longevity is the ability to heal yourself and live a long life independent of the conditioning of your past and that of family and society. You learn to live in *pure joy* with your partner in a conflict-free zone for as long as you choose by the power of your own thoughts.

Sondra asks the million-dollar question: Is your relationship lifting you up into more happiness in your life and sense of well-being or is it taking you down? You have to be the one to initiate the change if a relationship is not working. You have to be the one to take responsibility first for your part in any malfunction. You have to be willing to leave behind the old paradigm for relationships inherited from your parents and ancestors for a totally new model. So there may be a transition period from the old to the new. If you are reading this book thinking, "Oh my god, I really need to get out of this relationship" then you have to take a step. You may need to reconceive the relationship with mutual effort in a new purpose and frequency; you may need to change the form of the relationship with a new definition, such as "we are just friends now" or you may need to leave the relationship altogether, forgive yourself, and be grateful for the lessons it taught you. Sondra covers this very thoroughly in the section about transitions and forgiveness.

The difference between a holy relationship and an unholy or special relationship described in *A Course in Miracles* is the difference between the old paradigm and the new. When two whole people come together to share their light, the love is increased exponentially. Yet in the old model, we attracted a mate to complete, something we felt lacking in our self. This difference is made clear in the chapter on the old paradigm versus the new frequency. *Spiritual intimacy* is the key again to a closeness that is liberated from codependent motives of attraction and partnering.

For those single people who are seeking a mate, this book will prepare you to attract the right partner. You have to let go of the past. You have to forgive everyone and everything to make your aura radiant enough to attract the mate you want at a higher frequency than you are used to. Forgiveness is still the key to happiness, and this is the first practice to have the *spiritual intimacy* you desire beginning with yourself. This book will bring focus to the importance of forgiveness in your life and help you have the clarity to receive the partnership you want and deserve.

For those already in a relationship and want to improve or transform, the sections on forgiveness also provide the first answers and steps to *spiritual intimacy*. How can you be close to another you judge or to whom you hold a grievance? Forgiveness offers you what you want. You can reconceive your relationship to a new resonance of mutual respect and responsibility. Two people committed to peace through total forgiveness can meet together, liberated from the past in a vibration of divine love and appreciation.

Once the relationship you are committed to shows up, what do you do? What are the steps to keeping it on the high road to a perfect happiness? You need to ask yourself, with a mate or not, "What is the purpose of my life?" And also if you are in a relationship, "What is the purpose of this relationship?" If you are not together for the evolution of your souls, and the liberation from your past, and the extension of your sacred purpose in the world, then why are you together? This is one of the basic premises of having *spiritual intimacy*. You are both certain of your purpose here.

The ingredients to having a great relationship in the vibrations of *spiritual intimacy* are well described in the heart of this book. Self-love is important. Clearing the past is important. Deciding to be conflict-free is important. Having spiritual practices you do together is important. Having a spiritually honored sex life is important. Treating money in a sacred way is important. Teaching your children to awaken their own God-given potential is important. Sondra Ray covers these and provides a guidebook for you to transform you existing relationship or attract a new one. The intention is high. You can be in a loving, peaceful, productive, inspiring relationship through an intimacy that includes a spiritual life. In fact, it is the spiritual life that will give you true intimacy.

This life of *spiritual intimacy* starts with some basic premises. "Freedom is at the beginning, not at the end" so stated by the great sage, J. Krishnamurti, which means the vibration you establish in the early stages of a relationship determine the life of that relationship. One agreement that is most helpful to make is to be conflict-free. For both partners to state that they commit to a relationship with no conflict is a decision that comes with its own power; its own spiritual force to undo any minor, or even major, differences. Conflict destroys intimacy and promotes separation. You always have the opportunity to choose peace instead of conflict. This agreement makes the choice for peace inevitable, which creates a climate for *spiritual intimacy*.

To cap off the opening illustration of what people really want out of life and a relationship, whether he rose to realize it or not, Jim Morrison spoke a profound truth. What people really want is *something sacred*. What people really want with their mate is *spiritual intimacy*. Here is the path to this, the practical guide to having a new model for relationships. The practices and approaches in this book can and will lead you to the relationship you really want with your mate when applied. They will inspire and guide you to a place of greater happiness and fulfillment. They will lead you to the holistic approach. They will lead you to the integration of all levels of your being: spirit, mind, and body. They will lead you to *pure joy*. This is what I have with Sondra Ray, and you can have it as well with your partner in the inner sanctum of your own spiritual intimacy, what you really want with a mate.

—Markus Ray

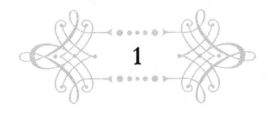

1

The Old Paradigm for Relationships

How does looking at the old paradigm of relationships lead to spiritual intimacy?

It has been said that he who does not study the past is bound to repeat it. One has to see clearly how one's parents had ego-based relationships (the old paradigm = the unholy relationship) and understand what that means, or else, one will unconsciously copy their parents' way. If you copy your parents' way, you are unlikely to learn what is a holy relationship as you will be merely stuck in the past. Subconsciously repeating family patterns you inherited from the past freezes the ego. The ego is a false self we made up to replace our God-created *self* and even God.

By looking at the old paradigm with your mate, you will wake up and see you do not really want that anymore. Looking at it with your mate is an intimate thing. When you face your ego together, you get closer and closer to the *truth*. A humble person recognizes his errors, admits them, and does something about them. To be humble in that way is a very spiritual thing. It requires an intimacy beyond just the sexual sparks and mental high you feel with a partner in the early romantic stage of a relationship.

How long do you think the romantic stage of relationships lasts on average? Couples want that feeling to last forever, right? Can you believe this stage lasts only around two months? I spent a long time studying why that is so, and I believe I found the answers. There was some very interesting research done in Minnesota at Hazelton

Clinic in the 1980s. They described the stages of relationships in the following way.

1. *The Dream Stage*

   This could be called the romantic period. It lasts only two months.

2. *The Disillusionment Stage*

   This is when one finds out all of the stuff they don't like about the other's behavior. She doesn't cook like your mother, he doesn't clean up after himself, he won't communicate his feelings, and so forth. This stage lasts, on average, two years.

3. *The Misery Stage*

   This could go on for thirty years! This is when the couple has been married for quite some time and all their negative conditioning and patterns (repetitive unconscious behaviors) have come up. Perhaps the children occupy so much attention that the pair cannot take time to clear or purify themselves. Perhaps the couple gets stuck in the "family mind" of their parents and cannot stop copying their parents. Perhaps money and sex issues take over. Perhaps health issues come up due to stress, etc. They get stuck. Then one or the other starts drinking, gambling, gaining weight, or having an affair for example. This makes them more stuck, and they go on putting up with misery.

4. *The Enlightenment Stage*

   This stage is when the couple stops blaming each other and starts looking within to change themselves.

5. *The Mutual Respect Stage*

   This is when the couple starts to admire each other finally! My problem with this research is that, by the time you get to the last two stages, you are too old to enjoy it! The first time I presented this research in a class, people raised their hands and said, "That is my parents" or older people said, "That's us."

I wanted to know how to go from the dream stage to the enlightenment stage and skip thirty years of misery. I became determined to find out how to do that. This study was one of the things that inspired me to create the Loving Relationships Training ®.

The five stages above represent the old paradigm. We need to examine the old paradigm carefully in order to *choose out* of it. The old paradigm is all about bad statistics. "Fifty-four percent of first marriages end in divorce, 67 percent of second marriages end in divorce, and 74 percent of third marriages end in divorce" (2000 US Census). Dr. Judith S. Wallerstein and Sandra Blakeslee in their book *The Good Marriage: How and Why Love Lasts* also report that 54 percent of first marriages end in divorce. They classify the remaining marriages as follows: 15 percent are truly romantically married and happy, 15 percent have become roommates and just cope, and 15 percent are actually miserable but stay together. This is a clear argument that the old paradigm is not working. A beautiful solution is needed.

The old paradigm is all about the following:

- Roles
- Domination and control
- Manipulation
- External power
- False security
- Codependency
- Projection of the past onto mate
- Blame
- Conflict
- Victim consciousness
- Conditional love
- Getting weaker

The old paradigm is full of upsets. The subconscious contains things from the past we are upset about, and these upsets are projected onto the relationship. Some of the subconscious issues that come up in a relationship are to do with the following:

- Birth traumas collide
- Family patterns dovetail
- Preverbal negative thoughts clash
- Past lives relive
- Death urges kill off the relationship
- Church dogma interferes

The couple usually divorces or becomes sick as a result of everything they have been suppressing.

On this subject, Markus has this to say,

"I can relate extremely well to the data Sondra cites above in the Hazelton Clinic report. I was in a marriage for thirty years and went through all of the various stages. The romantic period was short, the disillusionment stage went on for a few years, and then the misery stage kicked in and clouded our relationship for a very long time. We were both creative people, both artists; and for us, that combination was both good and bad. We had the freedom of a creative life, self-employment, etc., but also we struggled in many areas of our relationship. We often found ourselves at odds over money, sex, family matters, and the practical day-to-day affairs.

"The old paradigm contains conditions that inherently sabotaged our marriage. We were run by subconscious patterns of which we were not even aware. Each of us wanted our point of view to be right without seeing the perspective of the other. We lived much of our outer and inner lives in separate worlds and came together for meals, for entertainment, for sex, for an occasional trip in between the daily struggle of survival and work. I felt smothered and trapped in a prison, and she felt unloved and ignored by a mate who did not really want to be there. The years passed by, and we gradually grew apart. We never really discovered a frequency of spiritual intimacy even though we tried. We never discovered the conflict-free zone that is a decision two people must make in the beginning to have real marital joy. We never really joined at the heart and soul level. Our marriage was ill-conceived, and we were never able to reconceive it in a new frequency.

"We had our own spiritual paths and journeys amidst the struggle. In the beginning, we took them together, but gradually, these veered apart as well. I had a spiritual teacher whom I valued highly, Tara Singh, who gave workshops on *A Course in Miracles* around the country that I attended. She came to these workshops at first, but after a while, they became just my thing.

"We both had small businesses that kept us busy and preoccupied. We enjoyed making our artwork in our spare time, but somewhere along the line, the joy in our relationship had gone south. I found myself with a sense of futility and depression in my marriage. And because of my religious upbringing to think it was wrong to divorce, I stayed in a destructive relationship far longer than I needed to. It was destructive to both of us. So leaving it was an act of compassion to end our suffering together.

"Now that I have had the space to be out of it, I have arrived at the place of great respect for my former wife. She taught me a lot about myself by showing me areas where I needed to make corrections. We were both acting out of very subconscious thoughts that were running our relationship and producing undesirable results. It was a very creative time but also a destructive one. The old paradigm could go only so far because it was based on our old patterns of behavior we formed and inherited from our family, school, religion, and society. We had not really cleared ourselves of our birth traumas or our personal lies.

"No one taught us about relationships in school. No one sat us down and said these are the pitfalls to avoid or these are the common patterns in relationships that you must overcome. We blundered into each other, had a spark of attraction for whatever reason—both liked art—started having sex, moved in together, got married to mostly please our families, got involved with some way of making money, bought a house then proceeded to copy the patterns of unconscious behaviors passed on to us from our parents and ancestors. This was life in the old paradigm.

"When I met Sondra Ray in 1986, I came upon a force who planted the seeds of my transformation. She taught a seminar called the Loving Relationships Training® that made it absolutely clear how my old relationship was working or not working. It took me twenty years to integrate the information, but I could not ignore the various ways I copied my family patterns. I was not ready to leave my marriage because of what other people would think, or the guilt I would feel because my religion disapproved of divorce, or the fear I would have to face the unknown.

"In 1988, Sondra came up to me in a group rebirth in Hawaii, listened to my description of my relationship, and said, 'That marriage is killing you!' In fact, it was, but I needed to suffer a little more in the misery stage because my personal lie was 'I am guilty.' And all guilt demands punishment. To leave the marriage would have made me face that guilt and really feel it. It was easier just to stay stuck and miserable than to face the very thought form that was the cause of my misery. It was easier to pretend everything was okay. That was what my parents did for sixty years, so that was what I was supposed to do to be loyal to the family mind. I did not know there was another option, which was to be liberated from the family mind and the unconscious thought 'I am guilty,' and from all the misery this one thought attracted in my relationship. Finally, one day, I surrendered and said no to my suffering. I left the marriage to save myself and my wife from any further harm."

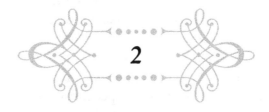

The Loving Relationships Training®

How does looking at family patterns lead to spiritual intimacy?

Family patterns are addictions. All addictions have to do with the ego. When you face the ego head on, you are going to be willing to let it go. You will see how these patterns have been running your old ego-based relationships. By acknowledging them and their tricky nature, you are more likely to choose out of them. When you and your mate choose out of these patterns, you are *waking up* and going for a more spiritual approach instead. You have to be willing to be intimate to discuss and face these patterns with your mate. You can avoid intimacy by keeping them suppressed, but you will never get out of them by not letting them come up to be healed.

Anytime you choose out of a pattern you are going for more holiness and more *spiritual intimacy* with your mate. It is a very necessary step in creating a relationship in the new frequency of *ascension*. You literally ascend when you choose out of a pattern. Your biology ascends. You receive more light in your mind. You get more excitement too in your relationship.

In the Loving Relationships Training®, we identify fourteen common patterns that keep people stuck in the old paradigm. These patterns seem to be the same in most cultures and also in homosexual relationships. The LRT® has been taught all over the USA, Europe, Australia, New Zealand, in South America, and in Asian countries. People easily identified with these patterns wherever we were. Our experience has been that people were glad to see the patterns clearly. It helped them realize what they had been subconsciously doing. A pattern is a repetitive unconscious behavior that results in tendencies.

I have always said for years in the LRT®, "Love brings up anything unlike itself for the purpose of healing and release." I was the first to say this in the original LRT® over thirty-five years ago, and it is just as true today as it was then. What this statement means is when you are in an intimate relationship and the energy of love is so powerful, it tends to push out of your subconscious all of your suppressed crap. These patterns are the main reasons people cannot stay in the dream stage of early romance. They get lost in the reactions of all that is unlike love and have no means of clearing them. These reactions just get stored up in the memory bank of the relationship until the resentment is so strong, it causes a breakdown or divorce. Here are the main patterns I have discovered are at the root of these reactions.

Pattern 1—The tendency to create a partner who is the same personality type as one of our parents

You have often heard these expressions, "he married his mother" or "she married her father." This is common because the mind seeks familiarity. But a woman could be married to a man who has the personality of her mother. Or a man could marry a woman who has the personality of his father. The point is which parent is your mate most like personality-wise? It helps to know this, especially because the tendency is to pick a mate who is like the parent you had the most trouble with! You would think you would pick a mate who was like the easier parent, but that is not usually so. This is because your higher self is trying to learn to forgive.

Another twist to this pattern is that one could deliberately pick a mate who is the extreme opposite of the parent they found most difficult. The problem with that is they will then subtly try to change the mate back into the difficult parent because that is what is familiar. There seems to be no escape from recreating parents until one gets enlightened and chooses to opt out of these patterns.

Pattern 2—The tendency to create a partner who treats you the way your parents treated you

If a parent abused you, your chances of attracting a mate who abuses you are high. This sounds insane, doesn't it? But we who teach the LRT® and have rebirthing/Liberation Breathing® practices see this over and over again. It is demonstrated that the mind seeks familiarity, repeating patterns ingrained from the family. Notice the root of the word "familiar" contains family, meaning of, or relating to, the family. If your father was critical of you, you are likely to attract a mate who is critical of you. You attract the thing you have not forgiven, and you are likely to keep attracting it until you learn complete forgiveness. Forgiveness is when you drop your grievance and the desire to get even. You chose to let go of blame. You decide to let the memory go. You cannot forgive partially. You forgive all the way or not at all. What it takes is a decision. The decision is to forgive and forget.

Pattern 3—The tendency to copy your parents' relationship to each other

Your parents were your models even if they were not good ones. Kids can't wait to copy their parents, but you may have looked at your parents' relationship and decided you did not like it at all, and so you planned to do something different. The odds are you will unconsciously copy their relationship anyway. It just comes out of you.

I know a young woman whose parents stayed married, but they had a fight every morning at breakfast. She decided at a young age that the way to stay together in a marriage must be to fight every morning. When she got married, she noticed she unconsciously would pick a fight with her new husband at breakfast!

Pattern 4—The tendency to attract and receive disapproval from one's mate due to the parental disapproval syndrome

The parental disapproval syndrome goes like this: Your grandparents disapproved of your parents when they were little. Your parents did not like it, but they each had a small body and a small vocabulary and could not talk back. They stuffed their resentment about their parents' disapproval and their inability to respond. When they had you, they took their revenge out by disapproving of you. You did not like it, but you had a small body and a small vocabulary, and you could not talk back to them either. You suppressed your resentment. You grew up and had children and disapproved of them. This pattern of concurrent emotions and actions goes on from generation to generation and becomes a syndrome.

The problem is that disapproval becomes associated with love, and we think love and disapproval go together. We get addicted to disapproval; that is, we expect it. So when we get into an intimate partnership, we dish out disapproval to our mate and children because we want to get it out of our system. We subconsciously expect disapproval from our mate since we have them set up as the disapproving parent.

All this disapproval lowers self-esteem and causes pain and withdrawal. Since it is a family pattern and has become a habit, it is tricky to stop. Only by becoming totally aware of this tendency as a pattern and consciously choosing out of it on both sides will there be a different result.

Pattern 5—The tendency to set up a win-lose relationship due to unresolved sibling rivalry

In a family with siblings, there seemed to be not enough love to go around. If one sibling got more love, it seemed like another got less. It never quite seemed like a win-win. Competition becomes the norm. This way of relating gets transferred to other relationships. We don't really know how to create a relationship withboth of us winning in a partnership. This pattern is strong in the workplace. It is called the invisible sibling syndrome. What that means is that you set up someone in the workplace to be your sibling, and then the competition starts, and the relationship is no longer relaxed.

Jealousy that started with sibling rivalry becomes exaggerated in intimate relationships. It is an open channel through which other destructive energies and activities can ride in. Having vicious thoughts about others can destroy one's intimate relationships.

Pattern 6—The tendency to get even and get revenge at parents by taking it out on another person, especially one's mate

All the suppressed anger one has for having received disapproval eventually wreaks havoc. The more you suppress something, the more energy you put into it! What do most people do with all that suppressed anger? They usually take it out on their mate. This is called projection. It happens really fast. Before you know it, you have your mate set up as your parent and you are dumping on them. This is the revenge pattern, and it is brutal.

Lesson 5 in *A Course in Miracles* says that you are "never upset for the reason you think." That means it is usually an earlier and similar event that gets triggered in you. You are reminded of what you are angry with your parents about, and you start getting even with them by taking it out on your mate. This is no fun at all, but it happens all the time.

Pattern 7—The tendency to remain like a helpless child waiting for your mate to take care of you

We did not feel like we got all the love we wanted as a child. We want to still be a child in the relationship and hope our mate will take care of us like we were never taken care of. The trouble is each one wants to be the child, and each one wants to be taken care of, so how can it work? If one does not get taken care of like one wants, more resentment builds. This ends up being the "will you take care of me" syndrome. People often stay in helplessness by starting sentences with "I can't" or "I don't know."

Pattern 8—The tendency to create struggle in relationships because having it easy and smooth is too unfamiliar and too threatening

First we had the struggle to be born. Then we had the struggle with our parents and struggle at school. We are used to the struggle. We may think we have to struggle to survive. We are more or less addicted to the struggle. If the struggle seems normal then having it easy would not feel normal. The strugglers meet the strugglers, and so they struggle together. People who have worked out the struggle pattern and have it easy meet others who have it easy.

I have known people who are scared of peace, scared of things being too easy. It is just too unfamiliar. The struggle pattern could show up in your relationship, in your career, in your sex life, in your body, or all of the above. It is important to see that we are making our own life hard by perpetuating the struggle pattern.

Pattern 9—The scapegoat pattern: the tendency to take out frustration on innocent family members

This is one of the new causes of divorce. A partner comes home very stressed due to work and or commuting. Then he or she enters the home and dumps all of his or her stress on innocent members of the family.

A. Goats were actually used in some societies of old where people pinned all their problems on the goat and sent it out into the forest alone to die, having taken on all the problems.

B. Don't allow this to happen to you. Don't become the scapegoat. Help your partner to release their stress in more appropriate ways.

Pattern 10—The control pattern: the tendency to need to always be right and in control

We have all been in situations where we feel no matter what we do or say or feel, the other person in our relationship has to always be right and in control. This pattern, or tendency, to be in control creates a situation where one person is dominating the other. This is not love.

A. This pattern is where one partner uses some force or threat and manipulation in the relationship. The other partner feels he or she has to walk on eggs. Controlling with anger is one of the most widely used method of keeping our partners "under our ceiling."

1. It is a big mistake to act as if the other person is put on earth to meet all your needs.

2. This control leads to darkness in a relationship, and the relationship is in danger of one party having a huge resentment that their voice is not heard.

B. The partner being controlled has to look at why he or she is allowing that and has to stop allowing that. He or she has to speak their truth without anger or defense and insist on being heard as an equal.

C. In short, never be under the ceiling of another.

Pattern 11—The tendency to channel the mind of blood family

There is a tendency to channel one of your parent's patterns or both of theirs. This is usually done out of love as an attempt to please the parent or to heal them. The principle is that children act out the subconscious minds of their parents.

You may take on some part of your parent's mind without realizing it. You may also take on their body type, which is a result of their mind. You may also take on their illnesses, which are a result of their mind.

In the LRT®, we look at how we are taking on our mother's patterns, our father's patterns, and the family mind in general. Then we ask ourselves what part of their minds are we copying or channeling in our life? If we are getting similar results in life that they did, obviously we are channeling their minds.

The solution is that one has to actually disconnect from each parent's mind and the family mind. You have to say, "I am *not* my mother. I disconnect from my mother's mind," etc.

In the actual LRT® seminar, we do this process. Complete the following sentences in writing:

1. A way I have been channeling my mother's mind is
   _____.

2. A way I have been channeling my father's mind is
   _____.

3. A way I have been channeling the family mind is
   _____.

Then we pair off with a buddy and share these findings with them. You can try this process with one of your friends, or even your partner if they are willing. People are always amazed at how loyal they are to the family mind and behaviors even if these are self -destructive! The first step of releasing the pattern is to look at it and breathe out the loyalty you held onto during the breathing session.

Pattern 12—The tendency to set up incestuous triangles because of unresolved sexual energy in the family

This pattern is the most insidious and the most tricky to handle. It has to do with *incest*, mostly emotional incest. This could occur when the parent of the opposite sex sets up the child or teenager to be the husband or wife. In other words, they channel romantic feelings toward the child/teenager that should be reserved for the partner/spouse. The parent may "over confide" in the child/teenager. The parent may send unconscious romantic energy to the child/teenager. The sexual energy in general becomes too strong for the child/teenager to process. This leads to sexual confusion later on.

Suppressed incest (meaning if we don't talk about it, it didn't happen) often stands in the way of physical affection. The point at which you could not receive physical affection from your parents, or they from you, is usually the point where your sexuality becomes inhibited.

The more your partner is set up as your parent, the less you will be able to make love to them because of the incest taboo. This pattern does not come up at the beginning of a relationship because it is suppressed. But it usually comes up after you move in with them and set up housekeeping or get married.

There is acted-out incest and emotional incest. Acted out is more prevalent than you think. This is when a parent or trusted caretaker crosses a boundary and inappropriately touches or molests the child sexually. Most people had some emotional incest, which is telepathic. This is when the parent or trusted caretaker is flirtatious or sets up the child to be the wife or husband and actually transfers romantic feelings toward the child.

With this pattern, you are often attracted to what is unavailable or what you cannot have. Some people tend to go for people that are married or already taken.

When you set up your mate to be your parent, the sexual attraction goes flat because you could not make love to your parent due to the incest taboo. Some people can have great sex before marriage, but after marriage, it all stops. That is because, after marriage, it is like being in the family at home, and you cannot make love to your family members. Then attraction to someone outside the relationship begins to happen because you can't have sex with your mate, and this adds even more separation to your sex life together. You end up not wanting the person who is available, your mate; and the person who is unavailable (someone outside the relationship), you can't have. All of this is part of the emotional incest pattern. Some couples may even end up sleeping in separate rooms as a result of this pattern playing out subconsciously. When one ends up in a triangle, one can be sure it is an incest pattern.

If one is attracted to a married man, for example, one is secretly trying to get Dad away from Mom. Some eventually throw in the towel altogether and get divorced because they never handled their incest issues.

Pattern 13—The tendency to punish oneself or get punished because of unresolved guilt

Guilt demands punishment. Let's say you have guilt for hurting your mother at birth, guilt from past lives, religious guilt, guilt for things you did wrong, and so on. Adding it up makes for a lot of guilt. Since guilt always demands punishment. Take a look at how you are punishing yourself. Are you beating yourself up at work or having someone else beat you up there? Are you beating yourself up in a relationship? Are you using your mate to beat you up emotionally or physically? Are you beating yourself up financially by losing money? Are you beating your body up with all kinds of aches, pains, accidents, or illnesses?

Pattern 14—The tendency to sabotage bliss and happiness

When you get a lot of love, peace, joy, aliveness, and beauty in a relationship, you often unconsciously try to get rid of it by sabotaging it with some underlying subconscious method. You may think you don't deserve it or aren't worthy of sustained happiness. In the LRT®, we say that when you have a very joyous experience, your response column comes up. That means anything unlike that joy and love will come up. That stuff coming up could sabotage everything. Being aware of this tendency is the first step to healing it. For example:

- Your death urge can come up and kill off the bliss, the peace, or even the whole relationship.
- Your personal lie (most negative dominant core belief about yourself) can come up and invalidate everything, especially invalidating your divinity.
- Your guilt could come up for having too much fun, and you will then sabotage things by punishing yourself somehow as guilt demands punishment.
- Right before you are about to gain something or win something, let's say get a raise or promotion or award, you could stop it from happening with this sabotage pattern.
- Or you could let yourself have the good thing but then think it is too good to be true, and so you mess it up afterwards.

The solution is learning to handle higher and higher levels of energy without going nuts. This integration can be done through Liberation Breathing® (conscious connected breathing), which includes lying still after each session and fully accepting the next level or frequency. One also needs to work on being innocent and staying clear of guilt.

One of the best, best ways of achieving spiritual intimacy is to do the 365 lessons of *A Course in Miracles* together. It will take you at least a year, but it is supremely worth the investment. I will write more on this later. You can also raise your spiritual vibration by reciting out loud the 108 names of the Divine Mother or going to India to an ashram. There are many methods of spiritual purification that help ward off sabotage, such as chanting, fasting, praying, and so forth.

These are the fourteen basic patterns we teach in the training. Why do we spend so much time looking at theses patterns? Precisely because your patterns do not go away if you avoid them. In the new LRT®, we provide processes as well as breath sessions that help people become liberated from these patterns. But even by reading this book and being honest about how they apply to your life, you are benefiting. Just seeing how they are running you is the first step in liberation from these patterns. These have to be owned and cleared in any relationship before spiritual intimacy is fully possible.

Not finding a relatioships training, which I needed, was one reason I created the LRT. Now I'll tell this story of another reason I created the Loving Relationship Training®.

Once when I was a child about five years old, my mom asked me a difficult question. I was somewhat of a channel, and so sometimes I could channel answers to her questions. This one however left me speechless. My parents had an agreement not to raise their voices in our presence, and so my sister and I were very lucky that way. However, they solved their problems behind closed doors in their bedroom, so I never learned conflict-resolution at home really. Once day, my mom came out of the bedroom, and it seemed she had been crying, so I figured out that they must have had an argument. She looked at me and asked, "Sondra, why do people who love each other the most treat each other the worst?" I tried to open my mouth and channel an answer, but this one was way over my head, and I simply could not speak. I never forgot her question however. Well, the whole LRT® is an answer to her question really, especially the first day of it when we clear the old paradigm. My mother was a teacher, but later in life, she was my student and came and took the LRT® from me. On Saturday, I looked at her in the audience and said, "Mother, this is my answer to your question when I was five."

Markus says this about the LRT®, which he has taken many times:

"For anyone who has taken the Loving Relationships Training®, they can never pretend again that they don't know how relationships work. It became clear to me from taking the LRT® that all these patterns I formed and inherited from my family and society were keeping me from perfect happiness, and that I better face them and choose out of them. Of course, they were in my mind, in my memory, but until I cleaned them out of my mind, they would still be programming my life. The most important thing that Sondra taught me in my first LRT® was that my thoughts produce my results in all instances, even my subconscious thoughts. There are no such things as idle thoughts, and at some level, my thoughts were manifesting something—positive or negative—all of the time. I lived my life through the filter of my thoughts and memories, repeating the same experiences over and over again. Inspiration is something very rare that happens in moments of absolute stillness and silence when my thought is not running me.

"The process of circular connected breathing in the upper chest, called rebirthing, which we now call Liberation Breathing®, is one of the main practices of release that Sondra teaches in the New LRT®. It is a gentle, non-invasive process that helps people integrate the material presented in the course and come to deeper understanding in themselves about their major life relationships—with spouse, parents, siblings, work colleagues, friends, and even to GOD. In this process memories and past experiences come up to the surface to be observed, forgiven, and released. Also, one can feel an emotional release and a deep sense of ease and joy from the session.

"The other advantage of the three Liberation Breathing® sessions in the training is that the body is rejuvenated. Taking in that much air can cleanse the cells in the body of old crud. Lying down in a relaxed atmosphere with the aid of the trained facilitators and assistants is conducive to letting go of the past—past memories of hurt, past traumas, past mistakes and regrets, and past relationships that are worn out. I found that this breathing process offered one of the easiest and most effective practices to release myself from my past. Coupled with other very effective spiritual tools, such as *A Course in Miracles*, Ho'oponopono, and alignment with the Ascended Spiritual Masters, the LRT® was one of the key experiences that transformed my life and continues to bring clarity and healing to myself and others."

3

How Your Birth Might Affect
Your Relationships

How does clearing your birth script lead to Spiritual Intimacy?

You probably wonder why on earth you have to look at your birth script to improve your relationship. Most of us had some trauma in our conception, pregnancy, birth, and after birth, which we call our birth script. I can tell you that your birth trauma is one of the biggest saboteurs you have going. But most people have no idea about that. That is why you have to look at it and study it. That is why we called breathwork "rebirthing" in the beginning because we were so clear that conscious connected breathing could get people in touch with their birth scripts; that people needed to rebirth themselves and go all the way back to their birth to clear these original birth traumas. Just a normal birth, in which you were perhaps handled roughly by doctors and hung upside down and spanked then separated from your mother, was a *huge trauma* that gave you a very negative first experience of life! The memories and decisions you made way back then are still active in your memory, replaying similarly in your life.

I had the privilege of doing some of the very first research on how one's birth affects one's relationship. Believe me, it is *major*. We were in bliss in the womb and really connected to the Source of all that is. When we came out, all hell broke loose, and we actually formed a lot of early preverbal negative thoughts (ego) at the time about ourselves, our life, and our relationships. These thoughts are running us, and most of the time, we have no idea of that fact since these are suppressed. So we are therefore operating from a negative thought system (ego) that does not serve us. When you and your mate start talking about your birth, it is a very intimate sharing. Surrendering to Liberation Breathing® to heal the birth trauma is even more intimate. I certainly hope I can convince you as to how much handling these changes everything. Read on!

In our Loving Relationships Training®, we study the circumstances around people's births and how those conditions influenced their view of themselves and life. Through the conscious connected breathing process called Liberation Breathing®, people get in touch with the preverbal thoughts they formed as early as their first moments of life in the womb and at their births.

While you may be tempted to skip over births different from your own, be reminded that you could be living with a person who had another type of birth you should know about. You can find out about someone's birth by asking them what they know about it. They at least know what number child they were, and usually, they know if they were wanted or planned. Their mother may have told them something else about their birth. Talking about the subject stimulates memories. It could be your mate, your child, your roommate, or someone at work you do not really understand. Your relationship with them may suddenly start to make sense after understanding the circumstances around their birth. Not all types of births can be mentioned here, but the following are the most common scenarios and their effects on relationships.

Conception trauma

Let's say your conception was unwanted, unplanned, or a mistake. People who were unwanted at conception may choose mates who don't want them. If conception was unplanned, or a mistake, then the conception of your relationships may be off, unconscious, or may be merely a chance encounter. Maybe you have never really chosen to be here if your parents did not consciously choose your conception. You may have thoughts like "I am not wanted" or "I don't want to be here."

Prenatal trauma

If anything unusual happened while you were in the womb, you may have wanted to get out of there quickly. You could have been premature as a result. If something very traumatic happened while you were in the womb like a car accident, you could have had a lot of shock and negative decisions, such as "I am not safe" or "I can be hurt." What if your mother smoked or drank during the prenatal period? This could have led to a toxic womb. If you did not like it in the womb and wished you were not there, you could fear entrapment in a relationship or resist it. You may need to demand space in a relationship. You may attract toxic environments or toxic relationships if your womb was toxic.

If it was wonderful in the womb and coming out was traumatic, you may want to go back! You could set up your relationship or house to be the womb and not want to come out. You may think it is unsafe to stay or unsafe to leave, depending on which way your womb experience went.

Painful delivery

If your mother had tremendous pain upon delivery, you could end up thinking you hurt women or people in general (primal guilt). This is mostly subconscious, of course, but you could develop thoughts like "I always hurt the one I love," and these thoughts produce negative results. You may shut down your aliveness because you think your aliveness caused your mother and others pain. You may have unconscious thoughts that you are bad (because you hurt your mother at birth).

Obstetrician syndrome

The obstetrician is the first person who physically supports, guides, coaches, controls us, and may manipulate us or hurt us at the same time. A person roughly handled at birth may become mistrusting of any form of authority figure or may even dislike positive support from a partner (if he or she is set up as the obstetrician). You may resent relationships that are at all like authority figures! Your mate might be trying to support you, but you interpret it as hurtful. This can cause a lot of confusion.

Most relationships play out the obstetrician syndrome one way or another. One partner is the rescuer, and the other is the rescued. One partner may be trying to fix the other. In order to be free of these confusions of authority in your relationship and be open to accept positive support, it is important to forgive your obstetrician completely.

Normal birth

People who had a normal birth often feel like they were no big deal. Sometimes they feel, since there was nothing unusual about their birth, they are not special particularly if other siblings had more dramatic births and received more attention as a result. If you had a normal birth, you may have thoughts like these in your relationships:

- I don't matter
- I am not special enough
- My life is just routine
- People don't really notice me
- I am boring
- I'm not good enough
- My life is mediocre

In some cases, you may feel guilty that you had it easy, so you cannot allow yourself to have it easy in a relationship.

Wrong sex at birth

Babies pick it up in utero if they are not the sex their parents wanted. We know this because of years and years of breathwork where people have had actual memories that their parents wanted the opposite sex. Later they may have the following thoughts, which definitely would affect their relationships.

- I am a disappointment
- I am the wrong one
- I will never be able to please people
- I should be the opposite
- I am not wanted
- I'm not wanted as the sex I am

You may have had difficulty with your gender and feel unaccepted. You could feel sad, angry, and resentful in relationships. You could feel your mate does not really love you for who you are. Perhaps you often cannot accept yourself in relationships. You may feel unappreciated by your mate.

Previous miscarriages, abortions, or fetal deaths

If there was a previous miscarriage, abortion, or fetal death in the family before a person was born, a good Liberation Breathing practitioner will always help you determine if that was the same soul that you are now. You can access this intuitively in a breathing session. Even if it was not the same soul, the mother would be fearful that the same thing could have happened to you, and this fear would affect your life greatly. If you were the same soul, I have found in my practice these tendencies:

- You could be afraid of life
- You may think people are out to get you
- You may think you don't want to live
- You may think that life itself hurts
- You often don't trust people in relationships
- You may not feel wanted or loved in a relationship
- You may feel like you shouldn't be here
- You may think you have to die in order to live, and you kill off projects and relationships before you come up with the right one

Held back at birth

Let's say the doctor was not there when you were ready to come out. The nurses may have tried to delay your birth or held you back until the doctor arrived. In some extreme cases, we have heard of the baby's head being pushed back into the womb and the mother's legs held shut in order to wait for the doctor or midwife's arrival. Held-back people may set up their mates or their bosses to hold them back and resent them for it. These are some common tendencies if you fall into this category:

- You often wait until situations get frightening or to a crisis point before taking necessary action
- You feel a need to break through a wall of resistance
- You may think, "I cannot get what I want, when I want it"
- You feel like others are preventing you from moving forward

Premature births

A baby intuitively knows it should stay in the womb nine months. If it comes out early, there was something wrong in there that the baby did not like. If the baby has to go into an incubator, it gets more complicated. A premature baby may grow up to have issues with time. You may have formed these debilitating beliefs if you were born prematurely:

- You may feel immature in your relationships
- You may feel vulnerable and weak in your relationships
- You may feel small and insignificant
- If you were an incubator baby, you may feel separate and alone in life
- You may be afraid of touch in your relationships
- You may feel observed and judged

You could have a kind of psychic wall around yourself that is not penetrable by your mate. That wall represents the incubator. Your mate might say, "I can't get through to my partner."

Caesarian

A Liberation Breathing® facilitator would try to find out why the client was caesarian in the first place. Was it because earlier siblings were caesarian? Was it a planned caesarian for some reason, or was it an emergency caesarian? Caesarians in general grow up with an "interruption syndrome." Their birth was not normal but interrupted. If you were a caesarian, these could be common tendencies:

- You may have a fear of or an attraction to knives
- You may think you cannot do it by yourself; that you have to be lifted out of situations by your mate

- You may resent others manipulating you
- You may crave touching
- You may be indirect in your communications
- You may tend to think you do it wrong
- You may find it difficult to make decisions
- Mostly, you may have a hard time completing things

Drugs at birth

If your mother was drugged at your birth, the drugs cross the placenta, which acts more like a sieve than a barrier. So you, as a baby, were drugged at birth and could have been born lifeless. These people could grow up and live in a fog. If this was your case

- You may fade in and out in your relationship or job
- You may feel unconscious in relationships
- You may complain of deadening your aliveness in relationships
- You may find it hard to focus
- You may feel ungrounded, disconnected in relationships
- You may feel out of touch and not present in relationships
- You may feel spacey in your relationships
- You may feel emotionally cold in your relationships
- You may enjoy drugs in your relationships and need to get high in order to be spontaneous

Induced

An induced birth is one in which the labor is artificially started, usually by intravenous drip. Sometimes there are medical reasons for the induction; other times, the doctor wanted to play golf or go on vacation. Often, parents wanted the baby to be born on a certain day. People who had induced births resent someone else telling them when they need to do things. They may have problems getting started. If you were induced, these could be your patterns:

- You may have a problem with time in general
- You may think your partner should do it for you
- You may feel helpless and wait for someone to serve you
- You may feel apathetic in relationships

- People or mates have to induce you to do things, and induce you to be in relationships; you often resent the induction
- Induced people often hate getting out of bed
- You may find others set up the rules and you feel trapped
- You may have difficulty starting projects

(My husband, Markus, was induced. But since we both practice Liberation Breathing®, we can talk about it openly. I say, "Now I am going to induce you to…" and then we laugh.)

Breech

Since a breech baby comes out backward (butt first or feet first), we as Liberation Breathing® facilitators would study why you, as a baby, chose to turn the wrong way in the womb. Usually, you were afraid to come out for some reason. These babies usually were afraid to face something out there. The birth was more painful for the mother and the baby. These people grow up and create a lot of struggle in relationships. You may notice these traits as a breech birth:

- You may back out of relationships when they get too close
- You might go into relationships and then fight to get out
- You experience pleasure followed by pain
- You may complain of people, or mates, trying to pull or force or manipulate you
- You may complain of not knowing which direction to go.
- You may speak of painful beginnings in life and relationships
- If your doctor tried to turn you in the uterus, you may have resistance to others trying to change you
- You may think you do things wrong
- You often go the wrong direction when driving
- Sometimes you may deliberately do things backward or against the grain of what everyone else is doing

Forceps

Babies born with the help of forceps have their heads scrunched, screwed, twisted, and pulled out of the womb. It can be very painful to come out this way. It is a highly manipulative procedure and often unnecessary. In the case of anesthesia, the mother cannot push, so often forceps are needed. Or the doctor may not have the patience to let the baby come out in his own time, so pulls him out with forceps. Imagine what it would have felt like to have your soft baby's head clinched with forceps! This was painful for you and was registered in your memory as one of your first and foremost traumas in life.

- You may grow up to have migraine headaches
- You may dislike being controlled or manipulated; however, you may set that up in relationships
- You may be more comfortable being in control
- You may think pleasure leads to pain
- You may often feel pulled out of situations or set up mates to pull you out
- You may fear you cannot make it on your own
- You may feel like your head and your heart are separate, i.e., disconnected to your feelings
- You may often fear touch

Cord around the neck

This one is complicated. It could even be considered that babies with the umbilical chord around the neck are making a suicide attempt at birth, and probably, they were hung in a past life. The "wiring" in their mind is convoluted. The source of their survival becomes an instrument of strangulation! It could create a primal schizophrenia toward life. They might grow up and have a love-hate relationship with life. Life and death become intertwined. The cord around the neck may result in these patterns if this was your birth script:

- You may be cut off from your feelings below the neck
- In relationships, you could have a push-pull time of it
- You get entangled in love as though it were the cord itself and then try to extricate yourself
- You may tend to create life-threatening situations
- You are very sensitive to feelings of being choked
- Intimacy can be risky business
- You often feel strangled in relationships
- You may even like crises

- You may find yourself saying, "This is killing me!"
- You may tend to sabotage your creations by killing off your creativity

I believe these people need a very experienced rebirther or Liberation Breathing® facilitator who can unwire their mind.

Twins

Twins can become more psychic and telepathic because they develop an intuitive connection to their sibling in the womb. If we are rebirthing a twin, their twin far away may experience what we call a spontaneous rebirthing. As breathing facilitators, it is important to study whether the client was the first twin out or second. If you are a first twin, you may notice these tendencies:

- You are out there first and often the leader
- You may experience guilt that you got to be first
- You may feel overly responsible for others' struggles
- You may feel you have to wait for others to catch up

The second twin out is often the follower. If you are a second twin then these may ring true as your patterns:

- You may play second fiddle in a relationship. You may expect your partner to lead the way.
- You may find it unnatural to think of yourself as first. You may always feel like you are on the back burner.
- You may find partners who grow rapidly and then leave
- You may feel an extreme rivalry in your relationships
- You may want a lot of space in your relationships
- You may have a terrible fear of closeness but may also crave it

In some extreme cases, there is an absorbed twin. One twin died in utero and was absorbed into the body of the other or into the body of the mother. Can you imagine how difficult it would be to be in the womb with a dead twin? The one remaining could have the preverbal thought, "In order for me to live, someone else has to die." Imagine how that thought would affect a relationship! If you are the mate, you could feel like you are being killed off or dying in the relationship.

When I was in nursing school, our class was shown a primordial cyst in a jar with formaldehyde. It was a ball with teeth and hair. I kept asking, "What causes this? What is it?" The answer the teacher gave was "etiology unknown." Now I know it was an absorbed twin, taken out of the body of the twin or the mother. Once I was rebirthing a twin whose sibling had died in utero. I suddenly started shouting, "Your womb was a tomb!" This is a very difficult case to handle, and the Liberation Breathing® facilitator has to be very experienced to help clear it. The suppressed guilt of the surviving twin could be very strong, and the breathworker must offer strong support in affirming the perfection of the situation, getting the person to see his or her own innocence that the other twin didn't make it.

There are many different types of births that can be unusual. We have had very interesting cases to study such as:

- Babies born in war zones, especially during bombing raids
- Babies born during natural disasters like hurricanes, tornadoes, earthquakes
- Babies born in taxicabs
- Babies born in elevators
- Babies born with the amniotic sac intact
- Babies born where the life of the mother and baby were in danger and the father was asked to choose which one should live
- Babies born from implantations, artificial inseminations from sperm banks, and modern methods of fertilization

You can easily imagine how much their lives would be affected by such incidents. The baby takes in everything already in the womb; what happens in the first few minutes upon coming out is crucial. Even the scenario around conception is very influential in a person's life. It is easy for a good Liberation Breathing® facilitator to find out how such incidents are affecting the person today. We are able to locate preverbal thoughts formed at the time of such conceptions and births. That is the miracle of it all. People get in touch with these unconscious patterns formed from their earliest life experiences and breathe out the negative charge. Through the power of the breath itself, a rebirth takes place. All of these negative issues can be cleared with conscious connected breathing in a Liberation Breathing® session.

In most relationships, the birth trauma of one partner often collides with the birth trauma of the other. When these issues are worked out, the whole frequency of the relationship changes and goes up! We have had people tell us in just three sessions of breathwork they have cleared issues they have been working on in traditional therapy for ten years! That is why we were guided to call this most recent form of breathwork Liberation Breathing®. Through the power of your own breath, you can be liberated from the negative thoughts and birth scripts that are adversely affecting your life.

There could be a number of factors happening at the time of your birth that weave together to form your birth script.

Markus has this to account about his birth and the conditions surrounding it:

"I was born in Hollywood in 1954. My parents were from Ohio, and they moved to California to start a new life when my only sister was one year old. My mom's sister and brother lived in the Los Angeles area, so she felt the support of her side of the family. Because my aunt Charlene's husband was a doctor and my aunt a nurse, my mom was advised by them to have me through a new method called induction. So on a Thursday evening, my mom went into the hospital; they gave her a drug, and I started to come out. My dad was at work, and my sister was with my aunt Charlene. I came out without making my own decision to do so. Because I did not get to decide about this, I felt much of my life that I was being induced to do things before I was ready or that I needed to do it myself to guard against others deciding my fate like at my birth. I became very deliberate about making my own decisions to the point of making them far later than normal or making them in rebellion in order to get back at the authority figures of my delivery team.

"But ultimately, I was responsible for the inducement. I did not want to come out of the womb for various other factors. My mom

50

had a previous miscarriage before me, and she was very concerned about my pregnancy going the full term. She ate extra vitamins and protein gelatin to make me grow and be healthy. I was very happy in the womb, but I could sense my mother's anxiety about my father's work situation. When they first moved to California, they were full of promise and hope. It took my dad awhile to find work, and they had to live with my aunt and uncle for a period of time. When my father did find work, Mom got pregnant with me and was concerned about another miscarriage and their financial picture. I picked up the thought, 'I am a financial burden' and did not want to come out. I was being fed very well inside the womb, so it made sense I would need to be induced to come out.

"On Saturday, Mom and I came home from the hospital and stayed a few days with my aunt and uncle and sister. Dad was not very present because he was working. After a few days, we all returned to my parents' apartment. I imagine a rather crowded place. Shortly thereafter, we moved to a bigger house but then my worst fear in the womb came true. My dad got sick with hepatitis, lost his job, and I was a financial burden. I felt guilt and failure about this because it forced my parents to give up on California and move back to Ohio. We all moved in with my grandparents in Mt. Vernon, a small town in the center of the state. My dad was sickly, in and out of work until I was four or five. Then at some point, things steadied out. He and my mom found regular jobs, bought a house, and settled into a stable Midwestern life a few blocks away from my grandparents.

"The family patterns around financial wellness had an impact on my life. I have always had what I needed, but I was often accompanied by an underlying anxiety around financial matters. There was a foreboding feeling that something would happen—the well would run dry, the bills wouldn't get paid, or no matter how hard I worked, there would not be too much surplus. I attribute this to my postnatal trauma of so much uncertainty about money in my early years. I did not link up coming out with success. So many of my major transitions in life, times in which I had come out had been fraught with financial instability. Thankfully, through Liberation Breathing, I have breathed out much of that trauma."

4

Personal Lies

How does looking at your personal lie lead to more spiritual intimacy in your relationship?

Your personal lie is the cornerstone of your ego. It is the one thought that invalidates your divinity right off the bat. This negative thought is a huge addiction. It holds you back, ruins your self-esteem, kills off your energy, destroys relationships, and leads to failure. All of that is the ego. Anytime you release ego, you are ascending and you are going toward more holiness. By cracking the case of your personal lie, you get more intimate with your mate and more intimate with God. By handling this, you stop invalidating your divinity and you start to *wake up* and get who you really are. It is really hard to be close (intimate) to your mate or with God when you are stuck in your personal lie. I know for sure this will become clear to you after you read this chapter. It is one of the most important chapters in this book, believe me.

Another thing that lowers the frequency of a relationship, or of any person, is what we call personal lies. A personal lie is the most dominant negative consciousness factor a person has in his mind. For most people who have never done a Liberation Breathing® session or rebirthing, it is totally subconscious. But everybody has a personal lie unless they are immortal masters who have been totally liberated from thought and the ego. It is a preverbal thought formed at birth, in the womb, or on some occasions, dragged in from a past life. This core belief seems real to the person and is one of the biggest sabotage issues running (or ruining) the person's whole life! Personal lies always begin with "I am…"

- I am not good enough
- I am wrong
- I am bad
- I am a disappointment
- I am a failure
- I am unwanted
- I am unwanted as a girl
- I am unwanted as a boy
- I am a burden
- I am guilty
- I am a fake
- I am alone
- I am not perfect
- I am an intrusion
- I am illegitimate
- I am ugly
- I am impure
- I am evil
- I am stupid
- I am slow

Note: We have uncovered as many as three hundred different personal lies and still counting!

It is our experience that each person has one negative thought about himself that is a lot stronger than others. It is important for us, as Liberation Breathing® facilitators, to help the client discover exactly which one is the dominant one, so we can help the person breathe it out and be liberated from it. A person has to forgive themselves for having this thought about themselves and be willing to see two things: (1) how this thought has adversely affected their life, and (2) how this thought is not the real truth of their identity; therefore, they can let it go and be totally absolved of its consequences.

Remember however, this thought is like an addiction. It is part of the survival script at our birth. It is one of the biggest ways we invalidate our divinity, our self-identity. Even though this thought has been the cause of a lot of pain, we have it closely associated with the coping mechanisms we have developed to survive. When it crops up in our results in life, we often get angry at people outside of us and blame them as though we are victims. Our lives cannot really work at an optimum level of spiritual intimacy until we locate and release this personal lie.

I will give you an example of how much a personal lie untreated can ruin someone's life. Let's take Michael Jackson. His personal lie surely was, "I am bad." He made a fortune singing and performing that song, and later, he became really bad, with drugs and children, etc. (What you believe to be true, you create.) He actually had two opportunities to get rebirthing sessions with me, but he did not do it. I feel sad about that as I think I could have helped him liberate himself from that thought.

Imagine how much your frequency will go up once you let go of your own personal lie!

Markus was well aware of the tendencies of anger and how his personal lie sabotaged his former relationship. In his testimony, he says,

"My first marriage was normal in the sense that we had our fair share of arguments, disagreements, and disappointments. My personal lie, 'I am guilty,' dovetailed with my former wife's personal lie, 'I am not wanted as a woman' (her parents wanted boys).

"These two thoughts were subconsciously suppressed when we got together but, nevertheless, playing themselves out in our relationship. I overcompensated for this feeling of guilt I took on when my parents had financial troubles. Coupled with the tendency to want to do it all myself from my inducement, I decided to be an artist and to be self-employed. But this underlying feeling of guilt would demand punishment, so I never succeeded enough to get out of the feeling of financial mediocrity. This would upset my mate, and I would feel even more guilt from her dissatisfaction with my mediocre financial production. Consequently, I would not want her affectionately, therefore, proving her personal lie true—I'm not wanted as a woman. This dynamic was so suppressed, we could not even see what we were doing to one another, and it went on for years.

"There is a way out of this. First, both parties must see which personal lie is running their life. Then they must see how each one's personal lie is creating behaviors that keep them locked in to them. That is why we call them dovetailing patterns. A dovetail is a furniture joint that is so strong, it cannot easily be pulled apart. The couple's dominant negative patterns lock together in a standoff, and both parties get stuck. But when you observe that is what you are doing and each takes 100 percent responsibility for his role in the standoff, someone, or both, can disengage from the battlefield. It is the purpose of a relationship in the new frequency to help each party free themselves from their personal lie. What can heal it is the exact opposite of the lie. It takes time however.

"I forgive myself for not allowing my former relationship to work. I was too convinced it couldn't. But from the ashes of the phoenix's rising, I got clear that my personal lie was the sabotaging factor. I was determined in my new relationship that I would free myself from the thought, 'I'm guilty.' For me, my first and foremost affirmation would be, 'I forgive myself for thinking I was guilty.'"

In the Loving Relationships Training®, we have two very important points that I must cover here. One is this, "Anything unresolved with your parents will come up in your relationships." The second is what I have already stated above, but is so important I will state it again, "Love brings up anything unlike itself for the purpose of healing and release.

These two things alone (plus all the birth patterns and the personal lie) should explain why the dream stage in relationships can only last two months. You get together and you are madly in love and the energy is very, very high. All this energy (love) you have for your mate penetrates them and stirs up the pot (unconscious) where a lot is buried that is unlike love. Your mate's love and energy for you is doing the same thing for you. It is like in beginning science class when you have a glass of water with mud on the bottom. You add more water (love), and all the mud gets stirred up. In this way, your mate is really healing you because you need to see what is down there. However, when anything unlike love is coming up, people usually don't handle it well. They fight rather than see there is a healing happening. What is on its way up is on its way out, but often, couples don't see it that way. They hang on to anger; it gets stored up as resentment and blame often suppressed, and the relationship stagnates and loses life. Welcome to the misery stage! Anger does not help the situation at all.

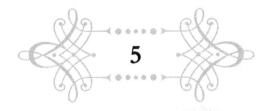

5

The Addiction to Anger and Conflict

I travel all over the world, trying to get people to forgive their parents and most do not want to. I give people this test: On a scale of one to ten, where are you at forgiving your parents? Ten is total and complete forgiveness for everything and zero is none. Five is half, obviously. People get very low scores in almost every country. I ask them to assign a forgiveness factor for each of the following:

- Mother
- Father
- Sibling with whom you are most upset
- Ex-spouse/and or last relationship
- Oneself

You can put a number there right now and take the test yourself. I try to explain that if they are not at ten on all of these, they are still angry. They may not be feeling angry in the moment, but it is suppressed. Then I go over the consequences of anger. Even after that, people still stubbornly refuse to forgive. As a former nurse, I can tell you anger of any kind causes circulatory changes. The heart rhythms are spiked. The smaller blood vessels contract into spasm, and the blood pressure goes up. My teacher Ammachi or Amma says, "Anger makes you weak in every cell of your body."

- It lowers your immune system
- It inhibits the digestive system
- Equilibrium is lost
- The entire organism becomes disorientated

- Ill health will be the inevitable result
- It makes you vibrate at a very low frequency
- It prevents you from reaching higher levels of consciousness

And perhaps the worst thing is this: it shuts out the mind of God!

The consequences go on.

Through anger and unforgiveness, much of the power gained by spiritual work on one's self can be lost! Your power gets drained. To carry resentment requires using up energy. It becomes an addiction. Research shows that the more often you are likely to get angry, the more you are affecting the neural pathways of the brain, and they go in a downward spiral. So then, regularly getting angry makes you get angrier! Anger actually makes a groove in these neural pathways. It is a kind of mental scar that keeps you stuck in repetitive, destructive patterns. Anger gives you a false sense of power and control.

Take the rageaholic for example. This person is striving for power and domination. His or her objective is to destroy any obstruction in the path. He or she is trying to utilize power to gain superiority. But really, their inferiority complex is such that they cannot tolerate an equal or superior. The angry people are the ones who are the most afraid.

But you might say, "I am not angry. I am just irritated!" *A Course in Miracles* says that every mild irritation is just a veil of intense rage. I made a list of different gradations of anger. Here it is.

- Irritation
- Being snippy or snappy
- Sarcasm
- Giving put downs
- Name calling
- Bitterness
- Heavy energy
- Grudges
- Covert hostility
- Resentment
- Defensiveness
- Revenge

- Meanness
- Yelling
- Verbal abuse
- Hate
- Rage
- Physical abuse
- Violence

All these kinds of anger have to be given up if you want to be enlightened. Anger and love cannot coexist. If you want to be healthy and happy, then there is no place for anger. Anger is the ego, and one should not be deluded into thinking that it isn't. There is no such thing as righteous anger. *A Course in Miracles* (*ACIM*) says, "Anger is never justified" (Text 30, VI 1:1). In *ACIM*, Jesus means what he says, and he says never! Why is that so? Because you are creating all the results in your life, and you are not a victim. Therefore, you cannot justify it. How did you attract that situation? You really have to read the whole *ACIM* to get this perhaps; but Jesus also says this: "You will attack what does not satisfy [you], to avoid seeing that you created it. (Text 30, IV 1:1) To attack means to get angry. In other words, you get angry at what you don't like out there rather than see you manifested it. But, you might say, your anger is justified because so and so mistreated you. Well, why did you attract that? Jesus also says: "Beware of the temptation to perceive yourself unfairly treated." (Text 26, X 4:1) This means that it is really tempting to think someone treated you unjustly; however, you attracted the way they treated you!

Arguing is always a manifestation of the negative ego. It is not the language of progress. It has been said that the smartest warrior is the one who does not fight. One should keep asking oneself this: Am I (or are we) ascending the ladder of holiness or descending? When you are angry, bickering, or arguing you can be sure you are descending the ladder of holiness. Whenever you engage in a negative encounter with another being, you are diminishing your own energies. You are pulling yourself down.

People get into the habit of bickering and arguing, and often, they rationalize it as being normal. But it seems to escalate until finally the relationship breaks because one cannot stand it anymore.

There is too much pain. Here is what some masters say on the subject of anger.

Guru Mai:

> "It is said that if you are a true ascetic, you are completely devoid of anger. If there is any trace of anger in you, you are called a scoundrel, not an ascetic. A great being will go to any extent to remove the fire of anger. The greatness of a saddhu monk is that he can drop something once he realizes he has it."

Dalai Lama:

> "We lose control of our mind through hatred and anger. If our minds are dominated by anger, we will lose the best part of human intelligence—wisdom. Anger is one of the most serious problems facing the world today."

Mata Amritanandamayi, or Amma, the Hugging Saint:

> "Anger and impatience will always cause problems. Suppose you have a weakness of getting angry easily. Once you become normal again, go and sit in the family shrine room or in solitude and regret and repent your own anger and sincerely pray to your beloved deity or Mother Nature, seeking help to get rid of it. *Try to make your own mind aware of the bad outcome of anger* (emphasis mine). When you are angry at someone, you lose all your mental balance. Your discriminative power completely stops functioning. You say whatever comes into your mind and act accordingly. You may utter crude words. By acting and thinking with anger you lose a lot of good energy. Become aware that these negative feelings will only pave the way for your own destruction."
> (From her book *Awaken Children*)

How do you get over anger and prevent conflict? You don't have to act it out to get rid of it. In fact, that is harmful to your body. Forgiveness is the master eraser of the anger. You have to forgive starting with yourself and your parents. A great criterion applied to spiritual maturity is whether we have forgiven our parents. In the mystic schools of old, a student was not even allowed in if he had not forgiven his parents. He was considered unteachable.

How do you handle anger then in daily life? Forgiveness starts dissolving it. It also helps to have guidelines for dealing with it while it is still coming up. Master Babaji gave me the highest teaching on this. I have never heard anything more effective. He said,

1. You don't stuff it. That hurts your body.
2. You don't dump it on another. That hurts them.
3. You change the thought that causes the anger, and you breathe out the charge. By charge, I mean your reactive energy that which makes you upset and disturbed.

Emotions are spearheaded by thoughts. You can say calmly, "The thought that makes me angry right now is…"

The way I deal with it is to say, "I am feeling activated." I can say that calmly out loud. That means I am not stuffing it, nor am I dumping it on someone. I am acknowledging it. I express the thought that is making me activated, and then I drop it. Or sometimes I make a joke to dilute the energy. I say, "If I was an angry person, I would be really pissed off right now!" To release the energy, one can run around the block several times, take a cold shower, get a Liberation Breathing® session and pump out the anger on the exhale, or do a spiritual practice to calm down.

Anger is an addiction, and the way we process addictions in the breathwork community is through this wat: you have to find out what the fear in giving up the addiction is. I often ask people in class what their fear is in giving up anger and conflict forever. The typical answers are these:

*   I could not defend myself
*   People would walk all over me
*   I would not be heard
*   I would lose all my power

- I would lose control
- I'd lose all my friends.
- I wouldn't get to be right

Let's examine these carefully.

I could not defend myself

This comes from a misunderstanding about defenses. People think they need defenses to protect themselves, but defenses (such as anger) are the opposite of safety. They are dangerous. *ACIM* says that defenses attract attack! By hanging on to anger, you attract more anger toward you, more attack, of any kind, coming at you. Therefore, it is important to master the lesson in *ACIM*, "In my defenselessness, my safety lies" (Lesson 153).

People would walk all over me

Actually people cannot walk all over you when you are in your spiritual power. Anger dilutes power and drains it although people tend to think anger is power. Nothing could be further from the truth; anger is a very false power. Peace is power. True power equals love, safety, and certainty. When you are experiencing peace, nobody can push you around. When you are angry, you are off center, and you can be further knocked off center easily.

I would not be heard

For many people while growing up, yelling was common. Those who yelled the loudest were heard the most, it seemed. So a person mistakenly learned that, to be heard, they had to be angry. This does not really work. People don't like to listen to others who are angry. The affirmation to change the pattern is, "People love to listen to me when I am loving and gentle."

I would lose all my power

Again it is a mistake to think that anger is power. Anger drains you of your power. Many men, in particular think they would lose their power if they gave up their anger. This is a misunderstanding of true power and a blatant trick of the ego. The ego wants you to stay stuck. The ego wants you to stay angry. The ego does not want you to become enlightened. The person saying this needs to redefine real power (love, safety, certainty). The person saying this needs to learn that peace is power.

What do I mean by love, safety, certainty? Well, love cannot really be defined. The best attempt to define it that I have heard was this, love is an all-existing substance noticed mostly in the absence of negative thought. Safety is what you feel in the presence of someone free of anger. Certainty is when you know for sure you are one with God.

I would lose control

Being in control is not something to be proud of. When we are in the ego with anger, we are controlling the life force and stopping it with anger. Control is very dangerous to the body. Control is very unattractive. It makes people want to get away from you. The mistake here is thinking our way is the best way. Control leads to darkness in any relationship. When we are controlling, we use some force of threat and manipulation. It is a big mistake to act as if the other person was put on earth to meet our needs.

I would lose all my friends

Angry people like to hang around other angry people, so they can blame and commiserate together. The person saying this is admitting that most of their friends are angry, so who would they hang out with if they stopped the game? This person needs to realize how many more friends of higher caliber they would have if they gave up their anger.

I wouldn't get to be right

This person has to ask himself if he would rather be right or be happy. People who always think they are right are annoying. They are usually control freaks and cannot stand anyone disagreeing with them. These people need to learn conflict resolution, which is discussed later in this book.

Markus's version on the consequences of anger:

"Sondra and I travel all over the world and see clients privately for consultations and breathing sessions. Anger and the consequences of having anger in the mind for long periods of time often show up in these sessions. Recently, we had two cases wherein anger played a major role in physical disease. Both clients had a lot of anger and unforgiveness toward family members; in one case, her dad, and in another case, her brother and mom. When we asked them to do the forgiveness test, they came up with zero forgiveness on these family members. They cited incidents from their childhoods in which they saw themselves as unfairly treated and hurt. Because of these incidents, they felt justified in holding grievances toward these family members.

"Both of these clients had bouts with cancer and were still struggling with the disease. As Liberation Breathing practitioners, we are trained to locate the causative thoughts that are manifesting as disease. Both young professional women clients had resistance in accepting the relationship between negative toxic thoughts and negative toxic results. Both of them refused to forgive and see their part in attracting these painful incidents with their family members. In other words, they were determined to hold on to their role as a victim and blame the others for their past woes. They had even attracted doctors who exemplified the same problematic relationships they had with their family.

"The obvious point here is that physical disease begins with mental disease. Thought always precedes form. Anger is a thought form that manifests disfigurement and conflict in the cells and determines their function and behavior. A healthy cell is full of happy thoughts. A sick cell is full of angry thoughts. Which would you rather have? The basic principle of metaphysics is that mind always determines physical manifestation. In the case of our clients, the grievances and judgments they held about their family members not released by true forgiveness were destroying their peace of mind and wrecking their health at the physical level as well.

"In both these cases, the consequences of anger in the form of cancer were clearly manifesting. Both women had very strong ties to the scientific world where mental precedents for physical results are not studied. Both had resistance to forgiveness; both were strongly critical of themselves and others; and both were, in essence, angry. At the end of their sessions with us, they did not want to forgive. In fact, they turned their anger toward us and left the sessions fuming! In their cases, you don't need to know rocket science to see the cause and effect relationship of anger to disease."

One has to be clear that one's fears of giving up anger and conflict are destructive and definitely are not worth hanging on to. By the way, anger also pushes away money and all the goodies.

"Have you moved up the scale yet on forgiving your parents? A great being will go to any extent to remove anger. It is a sign of greatness to drop something once you see that you have it. Why have I spent so much time on this subject? Precisely because you can ruin your relationship with anger and especially because you cannot get enlightened if you keep your anger!

"I will close this section on anger with a prayer from Yogananda.

May I Abandon the Anger Habit

O Eternal Tranquility!
Save me from attacks of fury fever
That shock my nerves and inflame my brain!
May I abandon the anger habit
That brings unhappiness to me
and my companions.
Let me not indulge in fits of selfish vexation
That alienate from me the affec-
tion of my loved ones.
May I never invigorate my resentments
By attentively refueling their fires.
O Queen of Quietude!
Whenever I am rage full, place thou
before me a chastening mirror in which
to see myself made ugly by passion
Let me not appear disfigured before others,
My face wrath-wrecked.
I would solve the difficulties of life through
Thoughts and acts of love, not of hate.

Bless me, that I heal anger hurts in myself
With the salve of self respect,
And anger hurts in others with
the balsam of kindness
May I realize, O Spirit,
That even my worst enemy is still my brother,
And that, even as thou lovest
me, thou lovest him

6

Leaving the Old Paradigm for the New Frequency of Spiritual Intimacy

Once I spent a week with Ammachi, and there was an opportunity to ask questions. Someone asked her this, "Why is it so easy to have friendships, but when it comes to intimate relationships, it is so hard?" Her answer was this, "Expectations and criticism." I thought about this a lot. Criticism does kill relationships. One reinforces what they consider the other's bad habit, and it then becomes worse, doesn't it? Of course, the ego is on a campaign to blame. Criticism is part of the parental disapproval syndrome.

In the old paradigm, there usually are bad habits of communication. There may be sarcasm, withholding, accusing, blaming, threatening, interrupting, mocking, discounting, judging, diverting, name calling, ordering, shouting, and so on. These are forms of verbal abuse and should not be tolerated. Other things that ruin the relationship in the old paradigm are infidelity, lying, addictions, self-destructive behavior, and violence.

A Course in Miracles teaches that no one is in your life by accident. No one is in your life without a specific purpose and learning goal. Some people are there for major lessons, and some are there for minor lessons. The lesson is always the same: to remove the fears and judgments that keep us from loving each other unconditionally. We have called each person and each situation into our lives. So then when there is a situation or person that upsets us, we need to say, "What is the lesson here?" This does not mean we have to accept the way a person behaves. But we do need to learn to evaluate their behavior and our reactions to that behavior instead of judging them. Nor does it mean we have to remain in an active relationship with them. It does mean that we still need to see that they are worthy of our unconditional love. *A Course in Miracles* says, "Every loving thought is true. Everything else is an appeal for healing and help, regardless of the form it takes." (Text 12, I 3:3)

When someone is behaving in a way that is disturbing to you, they are really asking for your love. When someone is asking for love, we need to give it to them.

A Course in Miracles makes us confront how we have handled relationships poorly. It makes us look at why relationships fail, why they are so difficult at times, and why we end up in pain with them. When I present the following in class, some people feel like they want to lie down or pass out! But later, they thank me. Even though reading this one section may be grueling, do not give up! In order to be able to assimilate the new frequency material later in the book, one has to get the old habits out of the way first. Without being willing to process your case, look at, own, and let go of your most negative thoughts or judgments, spiritual intimacy is not possible.

You are brave to face this in yourself. Whatever the fears, until these are confronted and released, these will cause us to continually manifest painful relationships and situations. Just before the anger section in my classes, I often write this statement on the board, "A humble person is one who recognizes his errors, admits them, and does something about them."

If you will go through this and choose out of it, your humility will start to shine through, and you can then become a candidate for the new.

A Course in Miracles has a lot to say about the old paradigm. They would call it the unholy relationship or the special relationship.

The *Course* says we want to be special and have someone who is special. In a special relationship, we regard one individual as more special than anyone else, more special than ourselves, and even more special than God! But this idea is a delusion. As children of God, all human beings together comprise the Sonship. In coveting one special relationship with one human being, we limit our love to only one small segment of the Sonship. And somewhere inside of us, we are inevitably aware that we have forsaken the totality of the Sonship.

This brings guilt into our relationship, and guilt houses fear. And love where fear has entered cannot be depended upon.

In the special relationship, we deny our need for God by substituting the need for special people and special things. Our imagined hope for salvation suddenly depends on one individual, so the attention our partner may devote to activities or people outside the relationship feels like a threat to our wellbeing.

An unholy relationship feeds on differences; each partner perceives that his mate possesses qualities or abilities he does not. On the surface, such a partnership seems to bear out the old claim that opposites attract. Upon closer inspection, however, a different picture emerges. In fact, each partner enters into such a union with the idea of completing themselves and robbing the other. They each remain in the relationship until they decide there is nothing left to steal, and then they move on.

In these relationships, what reminds a person of past grievances attracts them. Such people are not even attempting to join with the body of their mate. Instead, they seek a union with the bodies of those who are not there! What this means is that you tend to set your mate up as past people who were caretakers as I mentioned in the LRT patterns. So then you are not even relating to the person in front of you but to someone else from the past. How can that work?

The *Course* discusses what they call a special love relationship; and this, it says, is the ego's chief weapon to keep you from God. It starts with the belief that there is something lacking in us that can never be filled. We are incomplete. A person unconsciously says, "I can no longer tolerate how unworthy I feel." He seeks to find the answer outside. One embarks on an endless search to find satisfaction external to oneself. They seek to find a special person (mate) with special characteristics, and they fall in love with those who fill this need. This is the ego's version of a marriage made in heaven. As long as you, my special love, continue to act so my needs are met (and so I can avoid my guilt and inadequacy), I will love you. But if you stop meeting my needs, I won't love you. The smallest deviation from this arrangement induces terror. Thus we have placed our hopes for salvation on this one special person. Attention elsewhere is a loss. But this dependency breeds contempt, and we end up attacking those we depend upon. We also end up with guilt for using others to meet our needs. This guilt causes us to further protect ourselves since guilt demands punishment. In the special love relationship, our mate is supposed to be our savior or idol.

The *Course* goes further to discuss the special hate relationship. In this case, the responsibility for one's misery is shifted to another. We say, "It is you who has done this terrible thing to me." In a special hate relationship, the hated person's past mistakes are used to justify our attack. All mistakes are used to build a case against them. The ego's (ego = the false self we made up to replace God) plan for salvation here is centered on holding grievances. Anger always involves projection of our separation. Projection, while seeming to deliver us from our guilt, really reinforces it. Our guilt merely becomes strengthened as a result of our unfair attacks on another. The more we attack (get angry), the guiltier we will feel. The guiltier we feel, the more our need to deny and project. Our need to find scapegoats to hate is overwhelming. Having projected, we fear they will do the same. We unconsciously believe their attack back at us is then justified, so then we build defenses against our fear of retaliation. The problem then is that defenses attract more attack.

In these relationships, people are unconsciously chosen because of their vulnerabilities. Whatever reminds you of your past grievances attracts you. What you have not forgiven you attract.

The *Course* is saying that we believe we are separated from God, and that is a sin. But we don't want to face that, so we project that onto another (like our mate); now he or she is the sinner. The ego's plan for salvation is to attack the other person and see them as separate. When we threw away our innocence and took up guilt, we made everything a potential threat. We believe God is going to crucify us and demand our death. Then we have to defend ourselves against God. But we are going to pretend this is not happening. We now substitute our relationship with each other to replace God.

Let's go over this again. We have a shaky identity because we think we are separated from God. We have thoughts like, "I am not good enough," "I am weak," "I am a failure," "I am unworthy," "I can't make it," "I am not perfect," "I am bad," "I am guilty," "I am evil," "I am a fake," "I am nothing," "I am wrong," "I am a disappointment," and so on. As I said before, these thoughts are called personal lies in our breathwork community. Everyone has one. It is imperative to find out which one is yours

You become aware that something is bothering you, and you have to get rid of it. The way you get rid of it is attacking another (like your mate). At the same time, you want your mate to make you feel good about yourself, so you won't have to look at yourself. You want your mate to be what you need them to be, so you make them into an idol.

But in your mind, only certain people can meet your needs, for example, a brunette who looks like your mother. Your choices are based on the past. If your mate does not meet your needs, you think it is somehow okay to get angry. And yet *A Course in Miracles* says, "Anger is never justified." And Jesus means *never* when He says that.

This is the epitome of conditional love. *If* you don't meet my needs, I will hate you. But then I will feel guilty for using and abusing you in this way, so I will get more guilt and then more fear.

Pretty soon we set up a codependent bargain: "I am going to be dependent on you, and that means I can be helpless. You are going to take care of me, and that means you get to be dominant."

The ego's game continues in a special relationship. For example, "To make me feel less guilty, I am going to make you feel guiltier. By knocking you down, I get elevated. I want to be the king of the mountain in this relationship. I will become safer by dumping my anger onto you."

The ego led you to believe that what you do to others you have escaped. But you have to know the ego is savage and special relationships are brutal. Now you get more attracted to pain than to love!

The main problem is that we attacked our own identity. We got rid of God on some level, and we feel empty and alone. But we do not take responsibility for our own unhappiness. Our brother (mate or another) is responsible. We are looking for a substitute for God now, and that substitute is going to be a special relationship, which we feel will be heaven for us. We don't like the self we made because it is not special enough. We are mad at God because He did not make us special either. So we separated from God and made up our own world (ego).

We must now find someone else's specialness and take it. We have to find someone symbolically to play God, and they are to blame for our mess. This special person is supposed to save us, but when they don't, we get really resentful.

"[The] unholy relationship is based on differences, where each one thinks the other has what he has not. They come together, each to complete himself and rob the other. They stay until they think that there is nothing left to steal, and then move on. And so they wander through a world of strangers, unlike themselves, living with their bodies perhaps under a common roof that shelters neither; in the same room and yet a world apart" (from *A Course in Miracles* 1ˢᵗ Edition; Text; p. 435).

So we find this person, make them special, and they get to own our soul. We find this person who reminds us of the past. We set up a psychodrama that reenacts the past, and we think we will change the ending this time and get all the love we never got from our parents. The problem is when you rerun the past; it gets frozen. We are not really seeking love. We are seeking to fulfill our shaky identity. We have to understand that this plan will not work; it will only lead to misery. This is all going on at the unconscious level. That is why it is so tricky. That is why we need a teacher to point it out. That is why I am writing what I have learned from *A Course in Miracles*.

I suggest you read the material in the *Course* called "The Treachery of Specialness."

Take a breath!

Seeking a Mate

Let's talk about seeking a mate in the old paradigm. I offer this brief review of the old paradigm to help you get out of denial. Again one has to face the old before they can jump into the new.

The Problem?

Usually people get depressed about being alone; they get worried, desperate, or they give up. They may think they are not attractive enough, not good enough, or not wanted. None of this will work because it collapses the aura and introverts it. That takes away the necessary radiance for attracting a mate. The same is true if you are too disinterested.

When you have a problem finding a mate, you are still in control. You are stopping it from happening by the control you use to hold on to the above and related negativity.

The Answer

Forgiveness is always the answer. *A Course in Miracles* teaches us a new paradigm of forgiveness. It does not pardon sins because it does not make them real in the first place. It sees that there was no sin. We tend to try to forgive through the ego in the old paradigm. It goes something like this: you did this terrible thing to me, but I am going to be better than you and let you off the hook. The old forgiveness is condescending.

A Course in Miracles calls this false forgiveness. It seeks to pardon where it has seen wrongdoing. It thus becomes a subtle form of attack by a holier-than-thou attitude. "You are a terrible person because of what you have done to hurt me. I am an innocent victim of your unjustified attack. But in the goodness of my heart, I will forgive you anyway, praying that God will have mercy on your sinful soul."

The point is that what you see in the other reflects what you see in yourself. The *Course* says every loving thought is true; everything else is an appeal for healing or help regardless of the form it takes. We now see anew our enemy as our brother calling for help.

When we do not forgive, we are reinforcing their guilt, and in addition, we are reinforcing our own. The ego's plan is to have you see error clearly first and then overlook it. Yet how can you overlook what you have made real? By making it real, you cannot overlook it. If you look beyond error from the beginning, you then keep it unreal to you.

The Possibility of Love

Love is impossible where there is no forgiveness. The *Course* says that the unforgiving mind is full of fear with no room for love. It is sad with no release from pain. It suffers and abides in misery. It is torn in doubt, confused. It is afraid to go ahead, afraid of sound, and afraid of stillness. It is terrified of the dark but especially terrified of the light. It is angry and sees only sins. It wants to live but wishes it was dead. It sees no hope of escape. When you have an unforgiving thought, you make a judgment, and the mind is closed and cannot be released.

Furthermore, by failing to forgive, we are condemned to a seemingly endless cycle in which the past repeatedly recurs in the present. It could be called repetition compulsion, and as I said, what you don't forgive is what you attract.

Now see how different it feels when one does not make the sin real.

"I forgive everyone for whatever they did to me, and I know that whatever they did, I alone invited and now accept full responsibility for. I requested the lessons, and they helped me to learn that led to my further unfolding to light and love," or "I have made a mistake in my thinking to allow you to seemingly hurt me. I recognize you are merely doing what I invited and that neither you nor anyone can hurt me. I am only hurt by my own thoughts."

To forgive is merely to remember only the loving thoughts you gave in the past and those that were given to you. All the rest must be forgotten. Forgiveness is selective remembering. Forgiveness means release. It is that simple. To release something is to let go of whatever power it holds over us. *A Course in Miracles* would say that even our childhood situations were part of the Holy Spirit's plan to teach us forgiveness in the forms necessary for our learning. We must accept as true only what our brother truly is if we want to know ourselves. To the Holy Spirit, the effects of error are nonexistent.

The process of forgiveness according to *A Course in Miracles* has three steps:

1. Recognizing that what we have judged against in another is indeed what we have condemned in ourselves. The ego tenaciously holds on to past mistakes, using them against the other, saying, "I will never let you forget what you did to me." Your own suppressed guilt attracted your attack from them. (You were already guilty because you thought you separated from God.)

2. Understanding that you made them the guilty party represents a decision and is one that can now be changed. We have to want the shift. We have to choose to identify with our own real self. Say, "I have chosen wrongly, and I will choose again." Because we think sin is real in others, we think it is real in ourselves, and it is seen as unforgiveable. Therefore, our guilt cannot be forgiven according to the ego. If there is sin, guilt is everlasting.

3. Being willing to allow the work of the Holy Spirit since we cannot undo our guilt by ourselves. It is tempting to think we can undo our guilt alone without God's help. Instead, offer Him your little willingness to remove all fear and hatred and to be forgiven. The Holy Spirit can take away our guilt when we have withdrawn our investment in it.

Forgiveness and Our Wants

The following excerpts from Lesson 122 in *A Course in Miracles* show that forgiveness offers everything we want.

I. Do you want peace? Forgiveness offers it.

1. Do you want happiness, a quiet mind, a certainty of purpose, a sense of worth and beauty that transcends this world? Forgiveness offers it.

2. Do you want care and safety and the warmth of protection always? Forgiveness offers it.

3. Do you want a quiet mind that cannot be disturbed? Forgiveness offers it.

4. Do you want a gentleness that never can hurt, a deep abiding comfort, and a rest so perfect it cannot be upset? All this forgiveness offers you and more!

Why would you seek an answer other than the answer that will answer everything? Here is the answer: forgiveness is how you get out of hell.

Forgiveness and Our Happiness

Lesson 121 in *A Course in Miracles* offers forgiveness as the key to happiness.

I.   This is the answer to your search for peace.
II. Here is the key to having meaning.
III. Here is the way to safety.
IV. Here all questions are answered.
V.   When you feel that you are tempted to accuse someone of sin in any form, do not allow your mind to dwell on what he did. Ask instead, "Would I accuse myself of doing that? I will not lay this chain on myself."

A Course in Miracles talks about the forgiven world. In the forgiven world, there is spiritual intimacy with everyone because you see everyone in it as worthy of your love. In it, those you forgive totally will look beautiful to you. You will see the Son of God in them. How lovely is the world when you have forgiven God's Son!

Forgiveness frees one from the bondage of hate and heals the mind and body of disease, disharmony, and feelings of lack and limitation.

The central teaching of *ACIM* is that the way to remember God is by undoing our guilt through forgiving others and, therefore, ourselves. It is the healing of relationships. By going out to another in forgiveness, we are joining the Holy Spirit, and in our union, the ego's belief in separation and guilt is undone. The Holy Spirit asks us to see all things as lessons in forgiveness that God would have us learn.

The main point is that forgiveness of others constitutes forgiveness of ourselves, for it is our own guilt we see in them. This is a reversal of projection.

By facing the past, admitting it, and releasing it through forgiveness, we are getting ready for the new. We can begin to feel that we have control of our lives when we understand we are creating everything with our own thoughts.

Markus has studied *A Course in Miracles* for many years and had the good fortune to study seventeen years with a master, Tara Singh, who was trained by Dr. Schucman herself to teach the *Course* to the public. Dr. Schucman was the scribe of *A Course in Miracles*.

Markus shares here about this experience with Tara Singh:

"When I met Tara Singh at an Easter retreat in 1989, my life changed drastically. He blew my mind within a matter of minutes and brought to question everything I thought I knew. He took my little self I had so carefully constructed as 'me' and threw it in the trash bin. Then he introduced me to my true self, so much more grand than that former little me that I could hardly recognize my old self anymore. He did this through a natural process of spiritual intimacy was a way of life for him.

"Because Tara Singh had received his instructions in person from the scribe of *A Course in Miracles*, Dr. Helen Schucman, he had a direct power to transmit an energy that was very pure and profound. He could bring his mind to silence and stop a student's thought as well. A teacher like him is almost indispensible to undoing the ego, because we are so prone to self-deception in this area. We can think we are making progress when we are just putting a spiritual outfit on the same old made-up self. Tara Singh took me into a new frequency for relationships by totally wiping out this made-up self, my ego. His spiritual intimacy happened in the form of rigorous self-inquiry that reached the apex of attention. He would undo my conflicts along the way, which always climaxed with a release from the past. An awareness of deep peace would permeate my awareness in that moment. Often this peace would last for days. It was unforgettable.

"The workbook of *ACIM* starts with one of the most confronting lessons of all time. It says, 'Nothing I see means anything,' then in the next lesson, 'I have given everything I see all the meaning it has for me.' I have given meaning to my opinions, which I defend, and then feel angry and afraid when I sense these positions are threatened. In the old paradigm for relationships, this is the status quo. Two people seldom drop their opinions in order to come to one mind, one peace, and harmony. The old paradigm is based on differences and this premise: 'I'm right. If you don't support me in my opinion, you are wrong.' Or often to avoid argument, each decides to do his or her separate thing but still live under the same roof.

"Tara Singh got me to question my life. Was I living out of the fear of survival or was I having something to give? These are basic life questions Tara Singh posed to me. They became my questions that led me to the new frequency for relationships. In my old marriage in the old paradigm, these questions were not possible to ask and receive answers because the whole basis of relating contained insecurity, wanting to become something more improved, and accumulating more stuff then maintaining that stuff. Simplicity was not possible amidst these factors.

"My relationship with Tara Singh I considered to be holy and totally self-honest. He was not a man who suffered fools or allowed the casual. A meeting with him was always spiritually intimate, which means it was always urgent to be absolutely factual and true. A meeting with him seemed like a month when it was just a couple days. He pushed me to go farther than my 'little life.' He pushed me to be all I could be. In his frequency, in fact, time stood still. I felt total unconditional love in the midst of a cobra ready to strike down my illusions at any moment. The spiritual intimacy of my teacher totally revolutionized my life.

"When I stepped out of my old life, I left with two suitcases of clothes, a couple pair of shoes, a half dozen books including *A Course in Miracles*, and a set of fine German kitchen knives. I left all property and financial assets to my former wife. I also left behind all of my discontent, inability to communicate, and frustration that our relationship could not seem to grow into a new level of harmony and fulfillment. I was not in a place of blame, but I was sad it did not work out for either of us. We had been together for thirty years.

"In the new frequency of spiritual intimacy I have with Sondra Ray, 'deep ease' and no conflict stand as the cornerstones of our relationship. We are both determined to leave the mistakes of the past behind and ascend into a higher level of peace and harmony, certainty of purpose, and mutual sharing of creativity. What we want is what is described in Lesson 122 of *ACIM*, mentioned above, the dozen qualities resulting from the forgiveness so essential to spiritual intimacy, which are (1) peace, (2) happiness, (3) a quiet mind, (4) a certainty of purpose, (5) a sense of worth and beauty that transcends this world, (6) care, (7) safety, (8) warmth of sure protection always, (9) a quiet mind that cannot be disturbed, (10) a gentleness that never can hurt, (11) a deep abiding comfort, and (12) a rest so perfect it cannot be upset. These are the means and the ends coming together and our credo for being together.

"We are very clear that we do not need each other; we are whole by ourselves without a mate. We are very clear that the purpose of our relationship is a spiritual partnership and that we are together for the evolution of our souls. We are very clear that we have been given great spiritual teachings in this life and that we have a responsibility to live by them and walk our talk. We are very clear that forgiveness of our past mistakes is the key to our present happiness. There is nothing as wonderful as this spiritual intimacy."

7

Step One to Having Spiritual Intimacy

The Purpose of Life

I read once that the mother of a prominent actor told him the purpose of life was to have intense joy. (Imagine having a mother like that!)

My gurus in India told me the purpose of life was to recognize the supreme. They understood that we are here to learn to recognize ourselves and others as part of the supreme God. Knowing who you really are and living accordingly lead to intense joy. Our purpose here is to remove all the fears that block our true nature—love—from expressing itself. We accomplish this through human relationships.

Another purpose of life is to learn. Ram Dass once said, "You are here to take the curriculum." One should use one's case (personal issues) as a stepping stone. Our world here is a school, and we must never stop being students in it. *A Course in Miracles* begins by saying, "This is a required course. Only the time your take it is voluntary. Free will does not mean that you can establish the curriculum." And the aim of the curriculum is "removing the blocks to the awareness of love's presence, which is your natural inheritance." Our purpose is to learn we are love, which can't really be taught but rather realized through removing the blocks to knowing who we really are. This action of removing the blocks that we do in Liberation Breathing® is miraculous.

Yet another purpose of life is to clear our karma. Some good books about karma and relationships are *We Were Born Again to be*

Together by Dick Suthpen and *Other Lives, Other Selves* by Dr. Robert Woolger. Karma is the cause and effect of thoughts and memories. We come together in relationships to see these cause and effect patterns and to clear them up once and for all. This is achieved through spiritual practices done together that lead to the development of spiritual intimacy.

One of the main purposes of life is to serve humanity. This is, and will always be, considered the first and foremost duty of the mature soul. This is called karma yoga. A couple living in the new frequency will make this a top priority.

Then there is the purpose of dissolution of the ego. This is a step-by-step process of giving up separation and limitation, which leads to the experience of ourselves as divine masters. This in turn leads to liberation when one transcends the human condition. A being has an intense desire to know the truth, the eternal source. Our overriding desire is to discover this source of infinite love and to express this love in daily life.

The Purpose of the Relationship

The purpose of the relationship then is to enhance these very goals. Both partners must share this intention, or they will keep on dying and reincarnating until they get it. When a couple is united in the priority of God-realization in themselves, they are ready to approach real spiritual intimacy.

I have seen over and over again that people do not have a good relationship with life itself. How can they have a good relationship with another, especially a mate, if they are not clear on their relationship with life? I was lucky that my mother repeatedly said to me, "Sondra, life is a miracle." I got into the wonder of it all, the joy of it all, and as a consequence, the appreciation of it all as a young girl.

Clients frequently tell me they wish they were not born, or they do not like having a body, or they think life is out to get them, or they feel life has sold them a bad bill of goods. They seem to be victims of life instead of being into its wonderful flow and taking responsibility for creating a beautiful one.

Spiritual intimacy starts with your intimate relationship with life and your relationship with yourself. You have to love life, love God, and love yourself if you want a wonderful relationship. This is obvious, but some people forget it. Complaining about life is off the track. Life is energy. Life is God. Life is innocent. Life is love, and it will respond to you according to your thoughts. If you feel grateful for being part of the living, part of life, part of the mystery of it all, then you are a good candidate for a relationship. I have found over and over again that couples have a real vitality to their relationship when they are discussing their spiritual growth with each other and sharing that deeply. When this is absent, the relationship can be dry and eventually boring.

I hear this a lot, so I decided spiritual intimacy is what makes it really flow with aliveness, and I have found this is what people really want.

On the subject of life purpose, Markus says this:

"When I first started rebirthing and looking at myself, I noticed that somewhere in my mind was a thought, 'I don't want to be here.' It was a sense of deep discontent that my life was not fulfilled even though I was doing what I wanted to do, and that there was something or somewhere better for me. I was self-employed and felt like the ruler of my destiny, but this persistent feeling of dissatisfaction sometimes haunted a darkened corner of my mind.

"I am not a perennial malcontent, but something in me was always a nonconformist stepping to the beat of a different drummer as Thoreau wrote. When I heard Sondra Ray say the purpose of life was to become enlightened, to be liberated from the past, to take 100 percent responsibility for all of my thoughts, deeds, words, actions and results, I began to think differently about the purpose of my life. As an example, Sondra was one of the most dynamic people I had met, vivacious to the max, a walking example of joy in action. She had relationships all over the world; in fact, I could see she was a master of relationships. She introduced me to *A Course in Miracles*, Babaji and India, Hawaii and Ho'oponopono, the Loving Relationships Training, but most of all to a life on fire and on purpose. She prepared me to meet Tara Singh even though they did not know one another.

"For a long while, I thought art was my purpose in life. I studied art in college and received my masters degree in fine arts. I continued to paint in a studio for many years and take my creative life very seriously. I became very sensitive to my medium of expression and developed a sense of craftsmanship and beauty. But even this lofty endeavor fell short of the real life purpose. Because I began reading *A Course in Miracles*, thanks to Sondra, I blundered into Tara Singh, who was one of its major voices. He spoke of having a function in life, something far greater than a career or a vocation. I remembered what Sondra had said in the LRT®, the purpose of life is liberation. Taraji, in his own power and force, spoke of the same thing. He would say, 'The only art is the art of living.' Are you free from you internal impurities, misconceptions and prejudices, insecurities, etc? What you do with God is the only thing meaningful in your life. You have a function to make your life one with the higher will of God. That is life's only purpose. Oddly enough, that is consistent with the things you really want to do, so there is no sacrifice in it.

"As I studied with Tara Singh, I became more immersed in the principles of *ACIM*. Taraji was to me a living example of these principles in action. He encouraged us to dedicate some of our time to service. He inspired us to go to Mother Teresa's missions and offer our time and skills. For three years, I went once a week to help in a soup kitchen to discover the joy and privilege of service. I even used my building skills to construct some bathrooms for them in their mission house. The Missionaries of Charity sisters lived a life close to Jesus, serving the poorest of the poor. Like them, I discovered I had something to give, free of motives. My discontent disappeared, and I became quieter within as a result of this service work.

"I started to be really grateful for life. That was the key. There are really only two songs of prayer in this process. Either one prays for the inner correction of forgiveness to be released from negative thoughts that are causing discontent, anger, misery and pain, or one prays in the spirit of gratitude and celebration for all the beauty of life around us. In the end, there is only real cause for gratitude. All else is our responsibility to release and let go. The real purpose in life is to be in a state of pure joy, and everything else that is not that can be effectively released through forgiveness."

8

The New Frequency—The Holy Relationship

It is time for a new paradigm, a new vibration, a new way of doing things. The new paradigm/new vibration begins with you. You cannot stay the same and go out and rearrange things out there. We are talking now about the frequency of joy and the holy relationship.

To have spiritual intimacy, one must work toward getting enlightened. One definition we had for enlightenment at the very beginning of rebirthing was this: you are enlightened when you have certain knowledge of the absolute Truth. What is absolute Truth? The absolute Truth is that your thoughts are creative. Your thoughts produce your results. The Bible says, "As a man thinketh so is he." Negative thoughts telepathically attract negative results, negative people, and negative things. Positive thoughts telepathically attract positive results, positive people, and positive things. In other words, life presents to you what your thoughts are.

You can also say that what you believe to be true you create. Also, what you think about expands. (God adds energy to your thoughts.) Furthermore, what you say is what you get. Jesus said, "Thou art ensnared by the words of the mouth." In *A Course in Miracles*, he takes it further: "There is nothing that happens to you without you calling for it and asking for it." That does not mean you consciously asked to have an accident or an illness. But your subconscious attracted it.

As you change your mind, you change your experience. Nothing that happens to you is caused by actors outside yourself. You create your vibe. One kahuna (Hawaiian spiritual master) said, "Think what you want, because you are going to get what you think, whether you want it or not." To sum all this up, Lesson 253 in *A Course in Miracles* says this, "What happens is what I desire. What does not occur is what I do not want to happen."

How can one clear anything in a relationship unless both partners understand this truth? If either one does not get how this works, you can be sure he or she will be in victim consciousness. You cannot clear anything up if you think you are a victim of others. The mantra for a victim is "Why me?" The mantra for an enlightened person is "I am light, and I am responsible."

An enlightened couple in the new frequency will constantly evaluate the results they get and study what thoughts and words brought about those results. They will evaluate what thoughts they need to change, and they will both work diligently on changing them. This is not only fun. but to share this process with a mate makes the relationship have a vibrant spiritual intimacy that cannot be felt otherwise.

When we received the gift of *A Course in Miracles*, we got a higher definition of enlightenment. And that is this: you are enlightened when you replace the ego's thought system with the Holy Spirit's thought system.

The ego's thought system is this:

- I am separate from God
- Therefore, I am a sinner
- Therefore, I am guilty
- Therefore, I am afraid I will be punished
- Therefore, this fear is causing pain
- Therefore, I am angry I am in pain
- Therefore, I am miserable
- Therefore, I am getting sick
- Therefore, I am getting depressed
- Therefore, I am getting old and going to die
- Therefore, I die
- (Death is a result of a thought called the ego)

You could also describe the ego as all your negative thoughts that keep you from remembering that you are one with God.

The Holy Spirit's thought system is this:

- I am one with God (no separation)
- Therefore, I am innocent
- Therefore, I am safe
- Therefore, I can relax
- Therefore, I am pure love
- Therefore, I have perfect health
- Therefore, I am joy
- Therefore, I am peace
- Therefore, I am happy
- Therefore, I can live & thrive more
- Therefore, I am pure life.
- (Life is a result of a thought called God)

A Course in Miracles is a correction of religion, and it came straight from Jesus. It contains the answers to all problems. It is, in my opinion, the most important book in two thousand years. It teaches the difference between unholy and holy relationships. When a couple studies it together, they become enlightened together, and what other goal can give you everything? Reading the *Course in Miracles*'s lessons together and discussing them gives you the spiritual intimacy you craved to have. There is nothing like it.

As I said, the books describe itselves as a required course, i.e., we must learn the material sooner or later if we want to be enlightened, but we have free will to decide how long it will take us to learn it. We can wait five months, five years, or five to fifty more lifetimes. But why wait? What if learning it now would get you and your partner out of misery, suffering, or death? In the Liberation Breathing® communities we work with, we try to use it as the underlying foundation of our relationships.

The *Course* clearly talks about the old paradigm as the unholy relationship and the new paradigm/new frequency as the holy relationship. I have assigned *ACIM* to couples who were about to get a divorce but did not really want to. I told them to read it aloud to each other. This has worked! They became incredibly happy in their relationships as a result.

The whole point of *A Course in Miracles* is to show us how we have wasted eons of lifetimes in the wrong state of mind. Until we learn the right state of mind, our relationships will not work.

To me, *A Course in Miracles* is the best gift you could give yourself and your relationship. The full impact of it can only be appreciated by studying it directly. Reading every line (even if you don't understand it) is like eating spoonfuls of purified energy. The *Course* will teach you to see everything differently.

A Course in Miracles says we need the whole Sonship (all of God's children) because we cannot understand ourselves alone. We must be grateful to all our brothers; to know them is to know God. See your brother as holy. It is your job to accept him as he truly is (a Son of God). We must not react to our brother's errors as if they are real. If we make our brother's sins real, we are also condemning ourselves as we are all one. When we accept our brothers unconditionally, we open the door to loving all of humanity. When you choose to judge rather than accept, you are losing your own peace. When you meet someone without any judgment, you will have deep peace. You will have spiritual intimacy.

We must exempt no one from the love we feel. We need to be the blessing we can give. There is no way to have it except by giving it. Devotion to a brother leads to your mutual progress.

What you want for your brother is what you will receive. When all you want for him is peace, then you will receive peace. This applies to your partner too.

"When you meet anyone, remember that it is a holy encounter. As you see him, you will see yourself. As you treat him, you will treat yourself. As you think of him, you will think of yourself... Whenever two Sons of God meet, they are given another chance for salvation". (*ACIM*, chapter 8, section iii)

In other words, what you give you will receive. If you give out anger and resentment, you will get that back. When you give out forgiveness and acceptance, that will be given back to you. And the fruits of forgiveness and acceptance in your life are peace and joy.

So then it is obvious by now that I see *A Course in Miracles* as the foundation for the new frequency for relationships. If you study it, you will be way ahead of the game. If you postpone it, you are postponing your happiness. But one has to go through the resistance to change. The old mind will make up all kinds of excuses why you don't need to learn what is waiting for you in *ACIM*. You may think your life is going fine now, so why bother? But sooner or later, the ego has to be tamed. It will eventually wreak havoc in your relationships, body, or career.

Some people may think they don't want to have all this spiritual stuff. They think it's no fun. That usually is because we confuse spirituality with church dogma. When you separate the two, you start having fun. When you replace the ego with the Holy Spirit, you have fun. Spiritual intimacy with your mate is fun. It is not only fun, but it is rewarding, interesting, uplifting, beneficial, enlivening, rejuvenating, moving, and something you won't want to live without.

Getting the Mood Right

First of all, what is the atmosphere of the home in which you live? In his book *Why Is This Happening To Me...Again?!*, Dr. Michael Ryce says, "People deserve to live in gentle, loving environments where aliveness and delight and joy are the norm. Anything less is an insult to the human spirit." Part of that includes having a living space that is beautiful and impeccable.

If there are piles of stuff around and basic grunge, how are you going to feel uplifted? There really is something to feng shui and neatness. It affects the mind and the mood. It is an ancient Chinese system of aesthetics believed to use the laws of heaven (astronomy) and earth (geography) to help one improve life. It is a complex body of knowledge that reveals how to balance the energy of any given space to assure the health and good fortune of people inhabiting it. I suggest you look into it to develop a natural propensity for order and neatness.

Being a pack rat is holding on to the past. When you fixate on the past, the ego gets frozen and you stay stuck. Energy, light, and great music should be moving through the space. Why not make your living space a temple? For example, I have an altar in every single room including the bathroom!

I once had a boyfriend who was neater than I was. It made me nervous. I couldn't leave a coffee cup in the sink or one fingerprint on the glass coffee table. It was driving me nuts. I thought, "Maybe he is anal retentive or something, being so obsessed with order. Maybe he had harsh toilet training." I knew that criticism or saying this to him was not going to work, so I decided to interview him. I said, "Roger, I noticed you are a lot neater than I am. What is your mindset on this?" What he said to me was quite mindblowing. He said, "Oh, Sondra, it is very simple. Prepare every room for God." Wow. That was a higher thought than I had. So I went up to his thought, and he taught me to be impeccable. I am so grateful to him for this lesson.

How to Find a Mate

Let's say that your living space is sparkling and ready and you want a mate. The first thing is not to need one in order to be happy. You have to be happy with yourself first. (Never marry someone who is unhappy thinking you can get them over it. Marriage can accentuate all human problems, so marrying someone who is very unhappy or depressed is a recipe for disaster.)

Next, pray to God and the masters to bring your perfect mate. If you are not ready, it probably won't happen, so you have to ask God to make you ready. (You could have fear of love or intimacy that you are not aware of. The Holy Spirit will never add to your fear by giving you something you are afraid of.) Surrender your prayer to your master (Babaji, Jesus, Ammachi, the Divine Mother) or to God. This is the cosmic dating service! That is what I call it anyway!

Next, put all your energy into your spiritual path and service to humanity. This will help you find a spiritual mate who is on the path of enlightenment, one who can handle the new frequency in which spiritual intimacy is essential.

If this does not work, it means you are still in control, i.e., stopping it from happening by using negative thoughts to block it. You would need to go to a breathworker or someone who helps you process your control pattern. When you are into the flow, there are no restrictions and all is well. When you are into control. you are stopping the life force coming through by placing a negative thought into the life stream, which stops it and blocks your good.

In the new frequency, our choice of intimate partners is not determined by old images based on unfulfilled childhood needs. You choose someone with similar spiritual goals as the top priority. You can, of course, stay in the relationship you are in and re-conceive it in a new paradigm if both of you are willing.

In her book, *The Esoteric Philosophy of Love and Marriage*, Dion Fortune says there are three types of joining: sex, karmic, cosmic.

We all know what the sexual tie is. It might go something like this, "Oh, we have such great sex, let's get married." Too often it is a rush job, and later, the couple finds out it was not such a good idea. It is all about the lower chakras.

The karmic tie is when you are connected because of past life karma you have to work out. These relationships are for learning forgiveness and may not be long lasting. Not all relationships are meant to be long term. When the karma between two individuals has run its course, there may be nothing left to bond them together.

The cosmic tie is the one I asked for. This is when you ask your master to choose a mate for you, so you can do a spiritual mission together. After all, the master knows all the karma of a potential mate, the future, the astrology, and everything else. This is the true cosmic dating service. It certainly worked for me! I asked my guru, Babaji, to find me a mate as I did not feel I could afford to make a mistake as a public figure. Besides, I knew he knew everyone's past, present, and future, so he would be able to pick someone perfect to join me in the mission.

I had been *very* independent for years, however, and I had to open up. So I took an action. I bought four presents for a man and wrapped them up. (My roommates thought I was crazy). I did a mantra. I did the affiramation "I am so happy and grateful my perfect partner is here NOW." I wrote letters to my beloved as if he was here. Later when I went to Philadelphia, Babaji actually sent two girlfriends (who were devotees of His) to be there so I would not miss the chance. They said "Don't you get it? Markus is the ONE" I could hardly believe it was happening and I might have missed it had they not been there.

Self-Love

Spiritual intimacy has to start with self-love. If you do not love yourself nor allow yourself to receive love from God, then you will end up being too needy, a very unattractive state. If you are wrong with yourself, you will be wrong with your mate and others. High self-esteem is always the answer. When you have it, you trust yourself, your feelings, and your intuition. You have to know you deserve love and that the universe is on your side. You must be clear on the following thoughts:

- I love myself; I am a lovable person.
- I am highly pleasing to myself and others.
- I am highly pleasing to myself in the presence of_____.

To stay loving with another, we must stay loving with ourselves. The ability to love ourselves even when we make mistakes is important; this is an aspect of the feminine side of ourselves or the Divine Mother energy within each of us. You still love a child when he or she makes a mistake. Can you not also love yourself in the same way? If you do, you will make fewer mistakes in the future. When you start judging yourself, you get nervous and make more mistakes.

My husband and I try to say, "Even though I made this mistake, I still completely love and accept myself." It is all about knowing you are okay no matter what happens. A person with healthy self-esteem may daily say something like that and then move on.

The New Frequency Defined

One of the best definitions I have found for the new frequency, I learned from Gary Zukav in his book *Seat of the Soul*. He refers to a spiritual partnership wherein the couple is together for the evolution of their souls and they are committed to each other's spiritual growth. Too often I have seen one member of the partnership be threatened by the changes the other was making. That is not the new frequency.

Another definition I like is this: the relationship itself is a holy interpersonal environment for the evolution of two souls. This couple is aware of the deeper reason they are together.

For spiritual intimacy to work, the couple is allowing a higher vibration to flow through them (such as the Divine Mother). Equality and wholeness become a way of life. How many couples do you know that are just letting TV flow through them? That is usually not a high frequency.

This kind of relationship is about growth and forward movement. It is a process. Each celebrates the changes in themselves, which are stimulated by the other. They do not resent that the relationship or the mate is stimulating them to change. Each should want the other to become all that he or she can be and neither of them is threatened by this. In other words, you do not hold yourself back in any way, nor do you allow the other to hold you back. Rather, you use the help of your mate to propel you forward, to advance! Each enjoys empowering the other, but neither gives away his or her power to the other. Here is the rule: never be under the ceiling of the other.

Intimacy is now a path. Intimacy leads to transformation. Intimacy is so powerful because it brings up all one's fears to be processed. This is a good thing. When you both have a mystical purpose, such as enlightenment and the removal of fear (ego), personal needs are transcended. I am talking about a paradigm where two partners are striving for the spiritual adventure of exploring the higher possibilities of spirit together.

In this kind of relationship, each mate is authentically empowered and goes directly to God. (Men used to make money his god, and women used to make men god. No more!) In this relationship, equality is recognized and maintained.

In this healthy relationship, both support the other and take responsibility for his or her happiness and fulfillment. You don't get to say, "You are making me unhappy." It goes like this, "I am responsible for my own happiness and joy, and others are responsible for their own happiness and joy."

Markus comments on our relationship:

"Sondra and I had to make some important agreements. We both agreed to having what *A Course in Miracles* calls a holy relationship for the premise of our being together: 'Each one has looked within and seen no lack. Accepting his completion, he would extend it by joining with another, whole as himself' (first edition, p. 435). In other words, we were both clear that we did not *need* each other to be happy, but that our joining could move us higher in our ascension. 'He denies not his own reality because it is the truth. Just under Heaven does he stand, but close enough not to return to earth. For this relationship has Heaven's holiness.' We were clear that our relationship was dedicated to this holiness in all that we did together. We were clear that heaven on earth was our goal for being here through whatever inner transformation and outer expression that would take.

"The great twentieth-century sage, J. Krishnamurti, said, 'Freedom is at the beginning, not at the end.' Meaning whatever a relationship is founded upon will be what sustains it through all stages of its development. Beginning a relationship with the goal of deep ease and no conflict as its premise set the vibration of harmony in our hearts that would produce inner peace. This freedom at the beginning proved to be a chord of strength that could lead us out of any discord cropping up from our past. It tuned us up for a new vibration together. And because we had contact with the wisdom of the sages, Babaji and the Divine Mother, *A Course in Miracles*, Ho'oponopono, rebirthing and Liberation Breathing®, The *I Ching*, and a worldwide network of fellow spiritual aspirants, our journey together placed absolute freedom and liberation at the top of our priorities. We were responsible for our total enlightenment.

"The new frequency of spiritual intimacy for relationships is new in the sense that living in that vibration would require a total inner transformation. It would be revolutionary, something different than our old way of relating. The reason it is new is that we have not brought this elevated frequency into application. It takes miracles to do this. But we must accept that we are entitled to have miracles when we seek this new frequency above all else. Miracles require a shift in our basic perception. We have to give up all attack, defense, and grievances toward another. We have to drop our opinions completely and arrive at a still mind, one that does not defend a position about anything. A new mindset is required to have this stillness and inner peace. Sondra and I were committed to discovering and applying this new mindset in which heaven on earth is attainable.

"What does this mean for our actual relationships now? Either we are in a state of unconditional love, which has attributes that are pure peace and joy, or we are not. Conflict has no place in this heaven on earth. Struggle and strife, seeking and becoming, accumulating more stuff all come into question in the new frequency. Also, victimhood is no longer valid. We cannot blame results we don't like on circumstances we feel are *beyond our control*. In the new frequency for relationships, all are 100 percent responsible for everything that happens within them, through them, and to them. There are no accidents, and the qualities of one's thoughts are the governors of all related experiences. Experiences don't just jump in front of you by themselves. You drew them all in.

"Problems in life are the results of erroneous thoughts in every circumstance without exception. The key to erase these thoughts from our memory bank is in our own hand. Forgiveness is the key for this process of erasure. The wise kahunas from Hawaii called this process of correction Ho'oponopono—'to set right what is already right' and correct our mistakes. This 100-percent responsibility is one of the pillars of the new frequency for relationships. Practicing this together as a couple can invoke spiritual intimacy.

"Your mate can no longer be a cause for your unhappiness, nor are they the source of your love. You have within you the source of love; in fact, you are that. 'I am that I am' means you are both the source and result of love. So all that is not love is the part two people in a relationship needed to be addressed and erased through the process of forgiveness. Each can help the other do this in an atmosphere of safety and support. I am grateful for Sondra not making my case real. This means she knows that my issues are not my real self, and she does not give them power. In other words, she sees the mistakes I may be making but does not blame me or want to punish me for them. She helps me to see them in myself first, and then she supports me in overcoming them. In this way, I feel totally supported when I am going through my stuff. I do not feel judged but, rather, helped along in such a way that I can make internal corrections and return to inner peace and joy. A humple person recognizes his errors, admits them, and does something about them.

"The conscious connected breathing we now call Liberation Breathing® is one of the fastest ways to clear the mind of sabotaging thoughts. In the new frequency, one must recognize the cause and effect of thoughts held in the mind even if one is not aware of these. By breathing out these thoughts, one is liberated from its effects. Liberation Breathing® is a means of forgiving yourself for all of the painful and traumatic experiences you have had as a result of your thoughts. It is a way of connecting your breath with the divine source and invoking the power of forgiveness to transmute memories of past and present hurts to a neutral state of nonjudgment. When the thoughts are neutralized, they can no longer play out their karmic effects. This is the whole point and action of Liberation Breathing®. Conscious connected breathing is one of the major tools for being in the new frequency. Sondra has been one of its greatest champions for over three decades.

"Through Liberation Breathing®, correction becomes a natural and essential way of life. In a moment of upset or stress, the causative factors in the mind can be cleansed and released. A relationship in the new frequency makes correction a delight and a joy. Correction becomes liberation, not a dread, because it frees you from the repetition of unhappy experiences caused by toxic thoughts and memories. My teacher, Tara Singh, often spoke of the 'love of correction,' which is when you are willing to look within yourself and take responsibility for all the events in your life, especially those not producing good results. You are totally willing to change them. Forgiveness of everyone and everything, especially of oneself, is the great erasure of pain and suffering. *A Course in Miracles* provides this essential prayer for the new frequency.

> '*Forgive us our illusions, Father, and help us to accept our true relationship with You, in which there are no illusions, and where none can ever enter. Our holiness is Yours. What can there be in us that needs forgiveness when Yours is perfect? The sleep of forgetfulness is only the unwillingness to remember Your forgiveness and Your Love. Let us not wander into temptation, for the temptation of the Son of God is not Your Will. And let us receive only what You have given, and accept but this into the minds which You created and which You love. Amen.*' (*ACIM*, chapter 16, section vii)

"The love that can heal any pain begins and ends with forgiveness. Our true relationship with God is at the root of our true relationship with our self and our mate. It is free of illusions. It is our first love of spiritual intimacy, the ultimate inner communion.

I knew a healer once who defined intimacy as 'in-to-me-see.' God, seeing all in you with love and forgiveness, offers you the most powerful spiritual intimacy. With spiritual intimacy, this relationship you have with God is at the very center of all other relationships. In the new frequency with your mate, forgiveness becomes the main focus and function of the relationship. Love will handle itself, and through forgiveness, all that is not love will be washed away forever."

9

Good Ingredients for Spiritual Intimacy

What are the good ingredients for spiritual intimacy in a relationship? Here are some specific suggestions:

Sacredness

The couple must value holiness above all else. There is a devotional aspect to the relationship. The couple has an attitude of worship and praise. They take time in the morning, for example, to do spiritual practices, such as reading *A Course in Miracles*, praying, chanting mantras, or whatever their particular path is. This is part of their spiritual practice daily. It makes all the difference in the world really. This intimate sharing is more satisfying than anything in my opinion.

Absolute Divine Friendship

You must be as open and defenseless as you are with your best friend. You should be as relaxed with your mate as you are with your best friend. You should be able to say anything any time like you can with your best friend. You should be able to have as much fun with your mate as you have with your best friend.

Innocence

How can you have any fun or aliveness if you have not handled guilt? It is important to read about the ego's use of guilt in *A Course in Miracles*. Innocence is your natural state of being, and it is an arrogance to think that you are guilty for anything. There is a big difference between a mistake and a sin. Mistakes can be corrected while sins call for punishment and guilt. When you make a mistake, you are still innocent. Your willingness to see your errors and correct them is all that matters. Blame and shame smell the same, so if you are angry and blaming the other for a woe or if you feel guilty and are attacking yourself for the error, both are equally off. Your *real* self is always innocent no matter what, and that is what makes the love of correction possible. It is always safe to look within, see your errors, admit them, and return your mind to innocence. One of the most important ingredients of spiritual intimacy is to practice this love of correction with your mate.

Clarity

Clarity of consciousness is the best thing you could offer a mate and children. Someone who is clear is liberated from the past or at least they are enlightened about where they are. For example, they would know if they were stuck and do something about it. Someone who is clear is constantly trying to choose the Holy Spirit over the ego. When I am stuck, I admit it. I say to Markus, "I am clear I am stuck. I need to get processed and have a breathing session." Because we are both experienced breathworkers, we can do this for each other because we have surrendered to the other.

Absence of Conflict

In this new paradigm the couple is a *team* and is going for solution to conflicts. There is an easy way to solve potential conflicts, a method that I channeled called the highest thought game. The first step is that each person has to give up their position and their need to be right. Then they strive to receive the highest thought for a solution. The highest thought would be the most positive, the most loving, the most productive, the best for all concerned, and the one that feels the best in your body. Whoever gets the highest thought does not matter. The other gladly goes up to the highest thought. If I get it, my mate gladly goes up to my thought. If he gets the highest thought, I gladly go up to his thought. There is no competition about who gets the highest thought. Anyone could get it—a five-year-old might channel it. If you get two high thoughts and you cannot tell which one is the highest, you agree to go apart to meditate on it. But usually, you can tell which is the highest as it is a relief in the body.

Here is a very simple example. Let's say a couple is about to disagree on the subject of what you want for entertainment during one evening. He wants to go bowling. She wants to go to the movies. (Yes, some couples argue about things like this and many other things including which brand of orange juice to buy!) You apply the game and look at the options: (1) he could go bowling alone and she could go to the movie alone or (2) they could both go bowling tonight and both go to the movie tomorrow night. They could come up with another idea like going to a spa or staying home and making love. They keep going until you reach the highest thought of all of them, the one that makes both of them feel the best.

I teach this conflict resolution game wherever I go. Couples who practice it are feeling really good in their relationships. The trouble is that most forget to play this game. When a conflict arises, the old paradigm couple reverts to arguing, bickering, and blame. The new frequency couple goes for solution.

Willingness to Change

The couple with spiritual intimacy does not blame each other. When there is a potential problem, they are on the same side looking at the problem out there. Each uses the problem as an opportunity to make a change himself rather than demanding that the other change. Each can ask, "What do I need to learn from this situation?"

Getting Unlocked

In the new frequency, women become unlocked or freed up from not speaking up and men become unlocked from not feeling *feelings*. The woman is encouraged to speak up and the man is encouraged to feel feelings. The couple becomes unlocked from these roles and others.

Spirit-based

The relationship itself is a spiritual path because everything that happens in this kind of relationship is considered an opportunity to grow and improve. Romantic relationships in this paradigm are the fast track to God. The couple practices love for each other as a mirror for love of God. They rise above the system of obstacles and turn everything into a spiritual opportunity.

Openness

The couple is open to new standards—new energy—and is willing to allow the activation of the Divine Mother/Divine Father in their relationship. Or the couple invites the Holy Spirit into their relationship and allows that presence to be felt. It is a conscious decision daily to invite higher levels of spirituality into the relationship. This kind of spiritual intimacy has to be developed with your mate. You have to make it a priority. I will speak later of the importance of spiritual practices, but first you have to be open for something new to come in. One must of course have an intimate relationship with God first.

Togetherness

Some kind of daily spiritual practice is a must, and best if done together. At first you can keep it very simple. There is a lot of truth in the statement, "The family that prays together stays together." It is a prayer of togetherness more than anything else. You could make playing great music into a spiritual practice. Markus and I listen to Buddha Bar and classical Indian music together, which make us very high, especially during lovemaking.

Discovery

Discovering what your partner wants, needs, and desires and helping him or her get it makes you both happier. If you are really in love, you want to give your partner what he or she wants, and this is a source of immense joy. At the same time, you remember there is space for differences.

When I pondered what kind of relationship I wanted that would be very, very different from those in the past, I came up with the term "deep ease." I decided if I were to manifest that with a man, I would have to manifest it in myself first. So I meditated on that for about a year before I met Markus. Amazingly, when he came, he first said to me, "Let's try to achieve a conflict-free relationship." That was just what I had wanted! With him, I have learned other qualities that are so valuable, and I list them here.

Deep Ease

This is the quality the couple wants and manifests. No more walking on eggs around the partner. The couple is relaxed with each other at all times, and their deep ease radiates outward and can be felt by others. There is no worrying about whether you can say this or that. You can share anything.

A Transforming Nature

The relationship is not stagnant; the nature of it is continuously changing and transforming. It is about movement and growth, and this keeps it alive.

Nurturing like a Garden

The weeds are pulled regularly. Nothing negative is carried over to the next day. Living is by the principle in the Bible: never let the sun set on your anger. Everything is cleaned up every night before going to sleep.

Spiritual Purification as a Way of Life

The couple enjoys doing spiritual practices together such as Liberation Breathing, learning and practicing *A Course in Miracles*, chanting, doing mantra on mala (rosary) beads, meditation, and so forth. It is best to do these things together in the early morning after bathing and before going to work or to the computer. There are more detailed explanations of these practices later on.

Having a Mission Together

The couple senses what they are guided to accomplish in the way of service to humanity. They also see their work as a form of worship. They have what author/visionary Barbara Marx Hubbard calls "vocational arousal." They love their work. Marianne Williamson says, "Your address book is your ministry." I like that! My master, Babaji, says, "Work is worship and idleness is death." His formula for happiness is love, truth, simplicity, service to mankind.

Imagine what would happen if a couple decided right from the beginning what kind of mission they were going to accomplish together for the world and then they actually did it! This spiritual mission could be a joint career. But if already in different careers, they could still decide what kind of service they could offer together apart from their careers.

When people are deeply in love, their happiness can lead to a natural concern for the state of the world, and they want to do something to serve it. If the love is stale it might be because they lack this quality of service. It is never too late to infuse your relationship with this quality. It is not only a gift to the world but also a gift to the relationship. It gives the relationship real meaning. It is always wise to focus on something greater than oneself.

Missions are satisfying. Most people underestimate what they could actually do if propelled by a clear mission. It is a good idea to offer yourself a big stretch. This helps you grow and extend your goodness to the world. I once did a training called Evolution. I asked each person to pick a mission they were willing to do that was a big *stretch* for them, knowing that that would cause them to evolve. They stood up and told what they thought they could do, and hardly any of them chose something that was a real stretch. They stayed in their little comfort zone. Doing what you might be afraid of will make you evolve, I promise you. Doing the same old thing won't lead to much change.

Gratitude

Instead of saying, "I will be grateful when…," the new frequency couple is grateful for what they have and for whatever divinity is unfolding for them now. They go through their day looking for things to appreciate! Gratitude ignites one's desire to give! In the book *The Magic* by Rhonda Byrne, she suggests you keep a gratitude journal and write ten things you are grateful for every day. Markus and I have been doing this for six months, and the results are amazing. We have even experienced huge shifts for the better in our finances.

Respect

This is the foundation for the couple. They know everyone is made in the image of God. They keep focusing on the good qualities of their mate and magnifying those. They do not make each other's "case" (ego mind) real. Take into consideration how you would treat an honored guest, let's say the Dalai Lama. You would treat him with utmost respect. Doesn't the one you are supposedly in love with deserve the same treatment? Think about *that*!

A Spiritual Community

The couple participates in a spiritual community and does not demand their partner to meet all their needs. The community (such as the breathwork community) gives them solace and deep and intimate friendships. It is a mistake to think that just because we have a mate loving us, we shouldn't need any one else's support

Imagine belonging to a group of fabulous people who are all working on enlightened ideas together and helping each other to become healed, happy, and whole. I am not talking about belonging to a cult or commune. There is a huge difference between a cult and a true spiritual family. In a cult, one gives all one's power away to the leader and you also have to reject your blood family. In a spiritual family, all can aspire to be leaders together and you are expected to clean up your relationship with your blood family. Everyone helps everyone evolve. No one is in control.

I envision a paradigm in which you and your mate are part of a supportive group of people who empower you to become all that you can be. A community where you can sincerely and openly share the problems you are having in your relationship or with your life and get help with them. A great deal of pressure is taken off your relationship when you have friends you feel intimately close to, who nurture you, and keep you on the path.

Imagine being able to hang out with a group of people who are not indulging in negativity but who are experiencing their aliveness, innocence, and own magnificence. Imagine being with a group that wants you to prosper and express your Christ nature. We lovingly call this group the ohana. This is a Hawaiian word that means "chosen family who breathes together." This family is dedicated to life itself. We invite you to join us. We look forward to meeting you.

(See "Resources" at the back of this book for the community nearest to you. If there is not one near you, we can help you start one.)

Enlightened couples still have problems, but the way they solve them is totally different from unenlightened couples in an unholy relationship. Enlightened couples use self-realization techniques to solve the problems. This is a huge difference. This couple is diligently ending dysfunction from their past. They are breaking destructive patterns and creating healthy models.

It is an enormous gift to your partner when you do your own work to clear yourself. If you don't, you may well end up like many old people who have not worked on themselves—inflexible and ultimately stuck. As Markus stated above and I cannot emphasize enough, the holy relationship we refer to in the new frequency relationship is defined by *ACIM* like this, "Each looks within and sees no lack. Accepting his completion, he joins with another whole as himself. They come together and share the light with the world." Completion first lies in union with God.

Markus comments on the ingredients for spiritual intimacy in the new frequency:

"Rarely has there been such a step-by-step guide up the ladder of spiritual evolution as *A Course in Miracles*. My teacher, Tara Singh, called it a gift for all mankind. He went on to say that it was the greatest contribution America had made to the whole world, even greater than the democratic government imparted by the founding fathers. And he had been closely associated with the likes of Mahatma Gandhi, Jawaharlal Nehru, Eleanor Roosevelt, William O. Douglas, and other eminent beings of the mid-twentieth century, not to mention a close student of Mr. Krishnamurti. But yet, we have to have the ears to hear its wisdom and the determination to rise above our conflicts and beliefs. We would rather keep our point of view and opinions about others than come to wholeness of one mind and one life. A serious look would show this is true in intimate relationships as well. We continue to choose a life of strife and struggle over the simplicity of spiritual intimacy.

"Some spiritual practice is essential for couples in the new frequency. This is more than just going to church on Sunday to get a weekly dose of religion. In India, there is a term, 'sadhana,' which refers to a person's daily spiritual practice. Sadhana is a discipline a person takes on in order to purify himself to ascend the ladder of holiness within. It is not merely reserved for priests and nuns but meant to enlighten everyone at whatever station in life they find themselves. 'The goal of sādhanā is to attain some level of spiritual realization, which can be either enlightenment, pure love of God (prema), liberation (moksha) from the cycle of birth and death (Samsara), or a particular goal such as the blessings of a deity as in the Bhakti traditions' (from *Wikipedia*, s.v. "sadhana").

"It is important that a couple in the new frequency develop some sort of sadhana that aids them in their ascension process. For us, this is a daily practice of reading and discussing *A Course in Miracles*, mentally cleaning with Ho'oponopono, Liberation Breathing®; and chanting the *aarti*, a beautiful hymn from India chanted to Babaji; or reciting of the 108 Names of the Divine Mother. Also, we consult the *I Ching* (Richard Wilhelm translation, Princeton Press edition) occasionally when we are seeking guidance on a particular issue. In the morning, we go for a walk and repeat the name of God on our mala beads. (a string of 108 beads used in India to say mantras and prayers, similar to the rosary in the western traditions). On our way back home we stop at Starbuck's to have a cup of coffee and discuss our day. These are the practices we do, but you will find your own spiritual practices that fit your own personal makeup and daily rhythm.

"It is essential that your environment be conducive to spiritual practice, and this means that order and beauty are a must. Living areas can have artwork and fine but simple furniture. Bedrooms can have light and wonderful linens and bedcoverings. It is best to make the bed as soon as you arise. Then take a shower to be fresh and start the new day. Give yourself some space just to be quiet and do nothing. Spiritual practice does not mean to be dogmatic and rigid and obsessed with rituals. The things you do to connect yourself with God have to be joyful and uplifting to you. If they are not, then don't do them. But one thing is certain, this time in the morning is for you to *give* to yourself and to God, and it is great if your partner wants to do the same along with you. That is the best. This time in the morning together is the beginning of spiritual intimacy. Sondra and I would not think of starting our day without that connection to God and one another. Be sure to take a shower before your practice and be sure *not* to open the computer until after the practice.

"It is common in India that a room in the house is dedicated to spiritual practice. Often it contains an altar of some central focus of special holy significance. Space is made in the home for this sacred space to be set aside and used on a daily basis. It is the sanctuary of the family, and it is a place where anyone can go to quiet themselves and go within, especially in times of crisis. It helps to have a relationship with some spiritual master or masters. They are giving us all the help we can accept, so why not accept it it? Put a picture of Jesus or Mary or Buddha or Lao Tzu or Moses or the Divine Mother or Babaji on an altar. I would say Mohammad, but he did not want any pictures drawn of him, so there aren't any. But if your tradition is Muslim, you could have your favorite quote from the Koran written in beautiful calligraphy. Light a candle occasionally. This sacred space becomes the heart of the household along with the kitchen, which is also considered sacred space. Food is prepared with the reverence of prayer, brought into the meal by attention given to the divine that has provided for our nourishment.

"But all of this said about creating sacred space and time in your day for practices, the most important ingredient to spiritual intimacy is not a practice or a special arrangement you make in your house for worship. The most important ingredient is the quality of who you are inside, this very moment. It is a quality composed of characteristics whose sum total put you closer to God and to your real self. You must embody these characteristics in order to rise in your spiritual maturity. This sum total is best described in the manual for teachers in *ACIM* in the section called "What are the Characteristics of God's Teachers?" The ten characteristics are listed and discussed at length. One could say mastery of these characteristics would put one automatically in the New Frequency for Relationships, and for sure invoke the blessings of Spiritual Intimacy. They are :

1. trust;
2. honesty;
3. tolerance;
4. gentleness;
5. joy;
6. defenselessness;
7. generosity;
8. patience;
9. faithfulness; and
10. open-mindedness (*ACIM* Manual for Teachers, p. 4.).

"We encourage you to study these characteristics together with your partner and try to embody them. You may fall down at times and not achieve them but just pick yourself back up and try again. Always try again. And in this process of picking yourself up, together you will unwittingly notice that you are becoming much more spiritually intimate with each other, with yourself, and with all those around you.

"This is the best link I know for an online version of *A Course in Miracles*:   http://acim-search.miraclevision.com/std-second-edition-and-supps/."

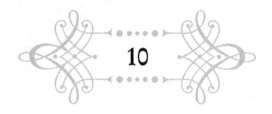

10

Communication Conducive to Spiritual Intimacy

Communication is everything in a relationship. Deborah Tannen's book, *You Just Don't Understand,* explains the difference between men's communication and women's. She shows how men and women have different purposes in communication. Women want it to be about joining and togetherness. Men, being trained to compete, use communication to be "one-up." Her research makes it necessary to be aware of this problem and to have guidelines and support in this area.

Communication is the key to keeping a relationship committed. I have heard over and over that people have affairs often because there was a communication breakdown in their marriage. Communication is to a relationship what breathing is to living. Of course, we are talking about mature communication that is respectful and loving. Loving communication is from the heart. It is almost palpable. It has an energy that changes the air around you.

When communicating with your partner, follow these suggestions:

- Commit to peaceful discussions.
- Know that you can disagree without having an upset (learn to use the highest thought game*).
- Do not withhold.
- Keep going until you both get satisfaction even if you have to take a break.

- Let go of your position while continuously looking for the highest thoughts.
- Go for a solution.
- Stay on the same side, looking at the problem together.
- Use words tenderly to help each other instead of criticizing.
- When tension is building, stop talking, hold hands, and ask to be connected to the Spirit. You can also read scripture aloud; *A Course in Miracles* is what I recommend. It works every time. The attainment of Spirit helps you transcend the negative ego.
- Allow room for differences to peacefully coexist.

*If it does not work for some reason, we recommend you get a third party such as a rebirther to help you decide highest the thought. In the new paradigm each knows when he or she is stuck. They can tell by the results. Results are your guru so to speak.

The Process of Clearing

Here is a very simple technique for clearing issues that come up. We call it the eight-minute process.

1. Set aside a private time for just the two of you alone in a safe place. It might be good to go to a very posh restaurant with carpet on the floor (to reduce noise) and very soft music.

2. Make an agreement to take eight minutes each to share. The one listening must be totally present and practice nonjudgmental listening. The one listening must be willing to follow these rules:

   a. Absolutely no interruptions
   b. Absolutely no making bad faces
   c. Absolutely no rehearsing of rebuttal
   d. Absolutely saying *thank you* at the end. I got it.

3. Then switch and apply the same principles. Sometimes you might need ten minutes. If the one listening gets acti-

vated (that is, gets upset or charged or angry), he must just breathe through it. The one who is sharing should try to use compassionate communication as taught by Marshall Rosenberg. Try saying, "What I observe is...," "What I feel is ...," "What I need is..." You don't get to say, "What I feel is you are wrong." That is not a feeling; it is a judgment.

4.   After all the cards are on the table. you can have a harmonious discussion with an equal give and take.

This process is simple, but you would be surprised how many couples don't do it. The ego is addicted to conflict and does not want peace. One has to be vigilant against the ego. If you win with your ego, you lose inside.

Imagine if each party said, "I want to use this conflict for what I can change in myself. I want to see this differently." Whatever comes up should be used for making internal changes. I learned this with my guru, Babaji. He would point out a conflict in my mind. Was I going to get defensive with him? No! Would I complain or talk back to him? No!

Your mate is your guru. They will bring up all your patterns so you can be healed. Be grateful to them.

The whole idea is to help each other obtain internal freedom as a result of the problem. Whoever gets the most conscious first should get the spiritual intention to get to a higher state with higher thoughts and disconnect from the battlefield.

I know a newly formed couple who went off to the Bahamas to get to know each other. I asked the woman how it went. She said it went badly because this man was unwilling to process stuff that came up. Now I have heard that the relationship is over.

What is processing? It is a form of self-inquiry which examines deeply the nature of one's unbalanced patterning. In the breathwork community, it is normal because we all know that a cleared consciousness is the most valuable asset.

The willingness to clear becomes one of the more important aspects in a new frequency relationship. When one partner is willing to do self-inquiry and the other is not, the combination rarely works. The partner willing to process usually starts to grow a lot faster than the other, and it soon becomes obvious that they do not share similar levels of commitment to the path. If you find yourself in a relationship like this, you need to look at how you created the situation and whether it is right to stay.

The spiritual master Yogananda has always said that self-analysis is the key to the mastery of life. He has also said that without self-analysis, man leads a robot-like life. "People who never analyze themselves are like mechanical products of the factory of their environment. They are preoccupied with breakfast, lunch, and dinner, working and sleeping, and being entertained. They don't know what they are seeking or why they never realize complete happiness" (Yogananda 1982).

The Bible says, "Be ye perfect even as God is perfect." That is an assignment! The only way to have a perfect relationship is if both people are willing to experience their own perfection. To experience your own perfection, you must be willing to release the ego's thought system.

Self-inquiry can be as simple as processing on a piece of paper or telling your mate the following:

1. My negative thoughts that created this situation are

   _____.

2. The desired result or outcome of this situation is

   _____.

3. The new thoughts (affirmations) I need to think about it in order to achieve the desired results or outcome are

   _____.

Giving and Receiving Feedback

Feedback is a delicate and challenging topic. Enlightened beings whose clear goal is total illumination usually welcome constructive feedback because they want to see their shadows as soon as they appear. The art of giving and receiving feedback occurs most successfully between people who have agreed to make it happen between them. In the new paradigm, this is established at the beginning of the relationship. You can open by saying, "You always have my permission to point out things that I do that do not work for you or that you believe could be detrimental to me or others. Do I have the same permission from you?"

I personally like feedback and welcome it. I especially like it from my teachers. It is one reason I am where I am today. In our spiritual community, we set up situations for this to happen formally and informally. A formal setting might be a seminar in which we are learning to increase our social or leadership skills. The group may suggest that someone could improve their appearance, speaking mode, attitude, or way of relating. The person who is receiving the suggestions is not allowed to defend himself or debate the feedback.

In an informal setting, such as a private conversation, we may spontaneously tell a person how we feel in their presence while not being harsh or critical. Some feedback I used to hear about myself was "Are you aware that you hang up the phone very abruptly?" I appreciated this feedback as I was absolutely unconscious of it. I then got to process why I had developed this habit.

In an intimate relationship with the person you live with, there is a risk of being less tactful, more critical, and too disapproving. This is because we choose mates who are like members of our family we are angry with. We take this latent anger out on our mates. Instead, how can we give each other feedback that is supportive, tender, and sweet? One agreement you can make is to give feedback on the feedback. "I can hear you when you say it like this, but I cannot hear you when you have that tone. It makes me shut down." The main point is to be sweet when you give feedback! And remember, criticism kills relationships.

Try this: Ask someone why they are doing something the way they are doing it before you criticize their action. Sometimes they have a very good reason, which refutes your judgment of them immediately. I wish I could always remember this myself. When you ask a question instead of making an assertion, it is much more gentle and often more revealing of the bigger picture.

Giving Feedback

Unless you have a prior agreement, the giver of feedback shall first get permission to do so by asking something like, "Do you mind if I share with you my feeling about…"

The giver shall not speak from anger or heavy energy. His heart shall be open as he if were speaking to his best friend with great respect. I will repeat this because it is very important: The main thing is to be sweet when giving feedback!

The giver of the feedback shall remember that the issue at hand could also be his or her projection. For example, if the giver says, "It feels like you are way too bossy." Maybe the other person, in fact, is not bossy, but the giver imagines this because his own parents were bossy or he is himself.

The giver should say, "What I feel is…and what I would like from you is…"

Receiving Feedback

The receiver shall keep his or her heart open and not become defensive. If the feedback is accurate, then he or she should be very grateful for it. If the feedback is a projection, it should not bother the receiver anyway. They can discuss it.

The receiver should pay attention if he or she gets this same feedback from more than one person. If so, he or she should take action to change it quickly!

The receiver shall thank the giver instead of defending or debating the topic. The receiver may wish to consider adding, "How do you suggest I alter this behavior?"

The receiver may take action by asking others to help clear this problem more quickly. For example, I said, "So and so said that I hang up the phone too quickly and cut people off. I do not want to do that. Please support me by telling me if you ever observe me doing that."

If couples can see that gentle feedback is a huge benefit, they will advance quite rapidly. If, however, the feedback is too critical, hurtful, or upsetting, it can be destructive in the relationship. People know the difference. How do you speak to someone you totally respect? How do you speak to your best friend? It helps to always imagine that your partner is your guru, your teacher, a holy person you are fortunate to live with! The main thing is to be sweet when giving feedback!

When something comes up such as tension, fear, clashes, and the like, the person who is in stress can say, "The negative thought I have right now that is causing my upset is…" It is that simple; then the one who is more conscious can help the other find a higher better thought.

Processing frees you from being stuck in the past and helps you cope with the challenges of life. Instead of avoiding issues, you look at them, play with them, see how you created them, and go for new solutions. The partner experiencing disharmony needs to recognize he is stuck and ask to receive help from the other to move out of the disharmony back into the connection and intimacy. The attitude of the listener should be "I am of service. How can I help?"

A Course in Miracles says, "Anger provokes separation. Communication ends separation."

Two people who practice forgiveness on an ongoing basis can usually stay together. Can you live by this statement: "I will not to keep any records of wrong doing"?

Markus's view on communication:

"Sondra and I don't withhold anything that is on our minds. Because we work together in everything we do, we are together 24/7 and need to be in harmony. Because of this togetherness, we can easily tell if the other is having something going on inside that needs to be discussed. Usually we will say to the other, 'Do you need a Liberation Breathing session?' And that is the key to taking time out and supporting each other through whatever we are feeling in the moment. We drop everything we are doing and go lie down and breathe.

"In Sondra's book, *Inner Communion*, she encourages us to reach higher states of communication in which the oneness of the universal nature of our source is known to us:

'Inner communion is being aware of what IS and being aligned with that all of the time; and not losing sight of the fact that that IS one's very center, one's core. It is ALWAYS there. IT does not go away. Communing with Divine Spirit is always possible; but we must first wake up to the fact that we have not been utilizing this potential. We have been turning away from the light or Spirit, by covering it up with our egos.' (*Inner Communion*, p. 33)

"In order to communicate well, there has to be a commitment by both partners to be aware of this inner spiritual connection. It is the basis of each partner's being, and the basis of the relationship itself. Sondra and I place our spiritual connection above all else. We are constantly in training to increase this connection in our awareness. We are not fanatics who get taken over by a single and confined belief system; we see this inner communion as a discipline to which we joyously give more and more attention. The result is more and more happiness, fewer and fewer problems and reactions. We become more relaxed and unpressured when we give attention to this inner communion. Out of this drinking of the divine in us comes a different kind of communication. We can have the space to be totally honest with ourselves. It is a joy to discuss things in an atmosphere of harmony even if we have slightly different views.

"Communication will make or break a relationship. We need a different way of relating wherein joy and happiness are the guardians of our minds no matter what we are processing or experiencing. In the face of a challenge, it is our commitment to harmony that keeps us in a state of deep ease. And if one of us slips into a funk or a reaction, the other is there to lift that one out of it by lending a compassionate ear that does not judge. We use the ultimate truth process: 'the thoughts that are making me feel this are _____.' We confess them and then go breathe them out of our mind. This way the dark cloud of any problem cannot stay around too long, and we are back into balance again. This is of course easy if your partner is a breathwork and/or understands the process. If not, you have to explain the importance of going to see a breathworker. Hopefully your mate will be inspired to do the same.

"Also, there are a couple prayers from *ACIM* we use to communicate this harmony to each other in the face of a challenge. Here they are

'Spirit is in a state of grace forever.
Your reality is only spirit.
Therefore you are in a state of grace forever'
(Text, Chapter 1, iii)

and

'God gives me only happiness.
He has given my function to me.
Therefore my function must be happiness.'"
(Lesson 66)

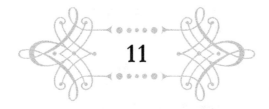

11

Duration

What is the duration of this kind of relationship? It is determined by how long it is appropriate and as long as they are still growing together.

What happens when one is growing and wants to be in the new paradigm, and the other wants to stay in the old paradigm? How can it work?

In the case when both people are not at all on the same page—or the same elevator!—the couple cannot see eye to eye or soul to soul. Separation is perhaps the best option. When one partner starts advancing rapidly, let's say through breathwork, and the other makes no forward movement, the levels or vibration will be vastly different. This could lead to breakdown due to the strain.

It may be necessary to sever ties even with other friends that no longer resonate. Maybe you can inspire them to go for a new paradigm, but maybe you cannot. Would you be willing to let go of your friends or even your partner if you knew that you would soon meet with higher-vibration people? I can assure you, higher-vibration people will come to you when you choose to go for the next level. If we let go of something or someone, new things and people do take their place though there may be a waiting period. You don't want to spend a lot of time with people who are miserable, do you?

Marianne Williamson wrote a beautiful prayer for a stressful relationship:

God, I place in your hands my relationship with _____.
May our relationship serve You.
May we see it with the eyes of love so only You might enter here.
You and I hold the truth of our connection as God created it.
We hold the truth of our inner awareness and oneness.
I invite the Spirit of God to enter here and dissolve any walls between us.
I forgive you and I want you to forgive me.

This way love will have the final word. We must learn to end our relationships well if they end. You either become bitter (failed spiritual test), or you become more loving as a result of that relationship (passed spiritual test).

Once I was in a good relationship (I thought) for two years. My partner came home one day and said "I have to leave." I said, "Are you upset with me?" He said, "No." I asked then "Are you upset with our relationship?" He said, "No, I just have to leave." So he left without any explanation. The same week, the house I was renting was sold, and I had to leave it. My car was also wrecked by a friend who had borrowed it. I lost everything that I thought was so important. I could not figure out at all how I had created it. I finally came to the conclusion that it was because I was going to India to find my master, and I had to go to the master naked. I was so proud of myself to figure this out that I took the bull by the horns and got on the plane feeling pretty good. But when I got to New Delhi, I started commiserating. I was really really missing my boyfriend and feeling sorry for myself. I was miserable. I suddenly heard a voice outside in the air, not even inside my head. (That has only happened to me three times in this life, and this was the second time) The voice said, "What if leaving could be a joy?" I started arguing with the voice, and I said out loud, "That is ridiculous!" Then the voice turned up the volume and said, "Just wait until you see what I have for you next!" I immediately fell to my knees in that park and I said "Pardon me for my lack of faith." And sure enough, I went to Babaji, and he gave me so much more than that little life I had thought was *it*. In fact, what he gave me was beyond my wildest dreams.

Markus reviews what his teachers said about relationships:

"My teacher, Tara Singh, said, 'All relationships must end in love.' That is a very wise thing to say but not always easy to apply. We often think that it is the other who is the problem. We think, 'If only they would change their behavior or drop their position, etc. our problem would be solved.' And then if they don't, we find grounds to blame the problem on them. Then we justify leaving because we are more reasonable, right, evolved, advanced, or elevated and they just cannot come up to our level. We tend to accuse the other and not see our role in making up the difficulty. Another one of my wise teachers of Ho'oponopono, Ihaleakala Hew Len, stated, 'Did you ever notice that when there is a problem, you are there?' Obviously, I am always part of the problem.

"If we could see that any problem we have in any relationship is because we have attracted it, contributed to it, played the major role in it, then we can stop blaming another and take 100 percent responsibility for all problems in our relationships. At first this seems drastic, but upon a closer look, this opens the door for complete forgiveness to enter and for the problem to be solved. If you make another guilty for the way the relationship has turned out, then you will not escape the suffering of guilt yourself. It will follow you around like a shadow until you stop pointing the finger of guilt at the other. In fact, there is no *other*, really. Whatever happens in a relationship you subconsciously or consciously asked for it to happen to teach yourself a necessary life lesson.

"Therefore, all relationships must end by seeing the other's innocence. Perhaps they showed you things in yourself you needed to correct. Perhaps they brought out in you your bad hair days. Perhaps they taught you what not to do in a relationship. All of these lessons were valuable for your own evolution. If you did not need the lessons, you would not have attracted them in the first place to act out the problem. So seeing a relationship through to the end can mean leaving it, but you end with a deep sense of gratitude for the person who showed you a mirror of yourself.

"I left a thirty-year marriage in which I made a lot of mistakes. But I hold my former wife in a state of great reverence for teaching me the lessons I needed to learn. I know it was right to end the battle in our relationship by getting a divorce. But I have no regrets for having stuck through a long period of struggle and strife if only to learn that I could finally say no to struggle and strife. I may not have been able to come to a state of peace and harmony with her in the marriage, but I forgive myself for that, and I am deeply appreciative of the quality time we did spend together. In this sense, I can say to myself that our relationship ended in love, and we are both innocent in the last judgment of our time together."

12

Are You Ascending or Descending?

When two people resonate at the same frequency, it does not matter what they do. It feels good, and it is fun. In this relationship, the couple is more interested in the vibration of God than their problems. Problems become opportunities. They rise above the system of obstacles. There is a feeling of cherishing going on. They are a cheerleader for each other's evolution. The frequency of chemistry can truly be felt when one is combining the wonderful energies of sexuality and friendship with the desire to use healing energy toward each other. In this combined frequency, the couple can heal each other; whereas in the old paradigm, couples could destroy each other.

A couple should cultivate their capacity to enjoy. There needs to be the intention of feeling good. Keep asking,

- Are we ascending the ladder of holiness or are we descending?
- Is what we are doing life-enhancing or life-depreciating?

If what you are doing is descending the ladder of holiness or is life depreciating, you are going to be feeling bad. If what you are doing is ascending the ladder of holiness and is life enhancing, you are going to be feeling good.

I hope I have made the point that relationships viewed from the soul level (holy relationships) are very different from those viewed at the personality level (unholy relationships). A relationship that is soul mated has a lot of passion naturally. One that is not soul mated may be lacking in passion, so that couple might create a lot of drama to get a rush. How will you ever get out of your karma that way? Your karma can bury you.

We must appreciate our intimate relationship because it inspires our heart to open and at the same time brings up our patterns left to be healed. An intimate relationship draws us out of ourselves. It can help us bring forth our finest qualities.

I see in my work that people really want spiritual intimacy. I see the joy in couples who are sharing that and communicating about that. Here is an interesting case study. I was giving a session to a woman who was a brilliant lawyer married to a brilliant lawyer. The more sessions she had, the more she shared she was totally bored with her marriage. She could not talk to her husband about her spiritual process at all. He was flatly not interested. Every session for eight sessions was about her desire to leave. After eight sessions she almost got the courage to leave but could not. Then she called me in a last ditch approach to save her marriage and asked me if I would give a session to her husband. I said I would, but I warned her that it does not work if someone does it to please someone else, and I was sure he did not want it for himself. Anyway, he came to his first session wearing an expensive suit, starched white shirt and tie—hardly the comfortable clothes to wear to a breathing session! I sat on the couch with him and began to explain the first premise of our work, that thoughts are creative and our thoughts create our results. He said to me straightaway, "I *don't* believe that." I said, "What? Sir, right here is where your marriage is stuck. You are not on the same page at all."

He did take the session and even had a good experience, but he decided he did not need that kind of introspection, so he never came back. She is now divorced and happily in a relationship with a breathworker!. She traded in her life of wealth for the simplicity and joy of having spiritual intimacy and spiritual communication. I know many cases like this.

Every relationship is a spiritual training course. Ask yourself these questions:

- Are you both choosing to be in gratitude, praise, and generosity?
- Are you regarding any situation that comes up as your teacher?

- Are you helping each other wake up and become all that you can be?
- Are you consecrating your lives to something sacred and holy?
- Are you creating heaven wherever you are?
- Are you in tune with the frequency of the most high?
- Are you constantly putting yourselves in situations that evoke your higher nature rather than lower nature?
- Is your life together as a couple a shining example of what is possible?
- Are you here to deliver God's vibes? (vibrations)
- Does the Christ presence within you commune with the Christ presence of your mate?
- Are you practicing unconditional love?

Unconditional love does not mean that you do not have to tolerate everything a partner does, but you don't stop loving them even if there is something you don't like. Conditional love is when you love them because they are fitting your personal needs, and if they don't do that, you stop loving them.

When you experience unconditional love, your DNA actually gets more orderly. There is a powerful intercellular resonance that takes place. There is a magic that can arise when two highly evolved beings begin to work together; there can be a strong electric current that flows between them and from them, especially when they are on the path of ascension.

The Path of Ascension

Ascension means raising your vibration and level of light. It is rising to a higher level or degree. It is a momentum, a gradual shift initiated by you. Ultimately, it is the transcendence of the third dimensional conscious awareness. It is a process completed with the merging of the physical body with the higher dimensional body, i.e., the Christ body—the light body.

The third dimension is about polarity, competition, containment, restriction, territorialism, thinking inside the box (or thinking within what someone else considers safe and established parameters), shunning responsibility. The fourth dimension is about time, infinity, endless possibility, trying this and that, healing the wounds of the third dimension, new modalities, becoming what you think is needed, and self-love (but still conditional); however, it still lacks integrity and the answers are not there.

The fifth dimension is where you want to go with your relationship and yourself. It is about total integrity, understanding, living true, unity, unconditional love, respect, doing exactly what you say, easy rapport, perfect health, turning up the light, and miracle consciousness!

Ascension to the fifth dimension requires a great deal of prior purification and preparation. Liberation Breathing® is a natural ascension path. It is blissful and liberating and should be your prime directive in the new paradigm relationship at this time. You serve as priest and priestess, initiating each other into the worship of the Divine Mother.

In India, they say there is nothing higher than worship of the Divine Mother. That is because the original spark of creation is a feminine aspect. The Divine Mother is the femine aspect of God. The original spark of creation is a feminine aspect. She is beyond the beyond. I have written extensively about this in my book *Rock Your World with the Divine Mother.*

In the fifth dimension, one becomes ageless and can even conquer death. If you stay in the third dimension, death is inevitable. In India, it is said that the Divine Mother can give you the blessing of physical immortality. Life is the natural state, and you have to become infinitely flexible in response to it. Life is either resistance or surrender. Resistance leads to suffering. Surrender leads to bliss. There is no room for death if one is saturated with life. (People die when the body can no longer clear itself, but now we have ways to clear the body.)

Death is hardening ourselves to the natural flow of evolutionary change (staying stuck in the old paradigm and the third dimension). It takes a huge expenditure of energy to keep the infinite away. It hastens decay and destruction of the body.

The masters suggest that you discard events or situations that throw you back into a space of heaviness. This may mean a complete transformation of lifestyle, but what better do you have to do with your life? If you are not giving your deepest consciousness and light, how will you feel complete? Offer your fullest radiance always. Ask to be overlighted by God and the masters.

Fear is the number one restriction to ascension. But you can breathe out that fear of change in Liberation Breathing®. You can call on the Archangel Michael. By choosing the path of ascension, you will have a great many blessings and great liberation. Think of things that will raise your light, such as generosity, singing, laughter, love, thinking well of others and doing them good, being out in nature, and so forth.

The power of a relationship in which both people desire and are going for ascension and physical immortality is awesome. The frequency that is transmitted from this couple's work together is a major healing contribution to the planet. The evolvement of the two will move quickly. You will know the relationship not only by its passion but by its deep ease.

Ascending happens through feeling (the feminine approach); it happens by extending love, praise, and gratitude to God and all life forms. As cells are filled with light and love, our consciousness rises to a higher degree. One is no longer controlled by the past. Cultivating the ascension attitudes of love, praise, and gratitude lifts one above the law of gravity where even death is unnecessary. Make ascension attitudes a moment-to-moment habit and a way of life. The closer we are to the Source, the more responsive we are.

In reality, all of humanity is on the path of ascension as evolution carries us onward and upward, *but* there is a vast difference between those who are consciously on the path and those who are not. Those who are conscious are functioning at a different and greater frequency. God realization is their reason for being. One becomes permeated with love, devotion, gentleness, compassion, and joy! I feel that ascension is the ultimate goal of spiritual growth. Imagine your mate as your ascension buddy!

Most people are holding on to old hurts or the past rather than ascending. But if your mate is your ascension buddy, he or she will help you let go of what is holding you back. I assure you, it is a lot more wonderful to have contact with the ascended masters than it is to block that relationship. You and your mate have to be willing to commit to changing any belief structure or situation that gets in the way of your growth or evolution. The problem you have to face is that your ego will divert you with all kinds of problems to distract you. At the same time, things you have been attracted to may seem different to you. They may seem a bit heavy and difficult to maintain. Upon ascension, you may even start to change in your physical experience regarding what you eat and drink and so on.

The first priority of ascension is to be of service. You will be able to do more and transmit a lot more love on this path. You will be given more and higher opportunities to serve. There is a lot of delight, and you can have a very enjoyable experience. Each will have their own unique experience. For me, life became like an amusement park!

Once your frequency stabilizes at the higher levels, you will have conscious awareness of a new level of understanding. The Bible says that "Ye who are grateful for *all* things, your body shall be filled with light and ye shall comprehend all things."

You can actually get off the wheel of rebirth and serve the masters at the highest level. Your goal is to become a spiritual master yourself. When you are on that path, you can manifest things more quickly. Ask your guides to help. Start now by living in a state of responsibility.

Say, "This has happened in my life. How have I allowed it into my life? What is the lesson for me? Then do something about it. Whatever happens, you start playing with it and see how you can use what you learn from it to serve others. The response to everything is acceptance, compassion, and unconditional love."

With spiritual intimacy, personal growth takes precedence, and the couples tend to live in solution consciousness. Solutions restore peace, and that is always a sign of spiritual intimacy, to be solving issues without conflict and to be ascending the ladder of holiness.

A Course in Miracles is constantly leading us to what Jesus calls the holy relationship. This is where both of you have consciously chosen the goal of holiness. You have both chosen the goal of peace. This gives you meaning and determines your experience. This gives two in the experience of being one. The moment of sharing is called the holy instant. You have to disconnect from the past and be open to a new way to experience things. Joining must come sincerely from the heart. When this happens, healing flows.

The meaning of this holy relationship is to transcend the separation. You are each other's savior. When you are truly ready to join in a relationship, you will find others to join with you. When you really want peace, you will find other minds to join with who want peace. When you are ready for this holy relationship, you will definitely meet others who are ready for it. You don't ever have to be alone.

If you have a relationship, place the relationship immediately under the care of the Holy Spirit. Invite in the Holy Spirit and his goal, then you will feel the spiritual presence guiding you in your relationship.

If you are trying to turn an old, unholy relationship into a holy relationship however, there may be a period of discomfort when the old structure and the new goal are at odds with each other. Do not lose faith. God has his foot in the door.

In the holy relationship, you see your partner as sinless. You see his incredible value. Faith will solve every problem. If a problem comes up between you, you must immediately disconnect from the battlefield, rise above it, stop talking, and invite the Holy Spirit in. Realize that the conflict is not about you and your mate. You are never upset for the reason you think. The problem is always in your own mind. All it takes is one of you to accept the holy instant. The holy instant is when you shift from seeing someone as your enemy to that person being your savior. It is choosing to see them as innocent. You enter fully into the present with no reference to the past. You set the goal of the Holy Spirit: truth, joining, forgiveness. You see that the whole journey is about forgiving one another. If I see my mate as the Christ, he or she becomes aware of the Christ within.

Here is an exercise from Lesson 78 in *A Course in Miracles*:

"Begin by holding someone who is difficult in your mind as you now consider him. Review his faults, the difficulties you have had with him, the pain he has caused you, his or her neglect, all the little and larger hurts he or she has caused. Regard his or her body with its flaws and better points. Think of his or her mistakes and sins.

Let us ask of the Holy Spirit who knows this son of God in his reality and truth that we may look on him in a different way and see our Savior shining in the light of true forgiveness given unto us. Visualize this.

Say, Let me behold my Savior in this one you have appointed as the one for me to ask to lead me to the holy light in which he stands that I may join with him. You stand with me in the light (say the person's name). The light in you is all that I would see (say the person's name)."

The central teaching of *ACIM* is that the way to remember God is through forgiving others and, therefore, ourselves. In healing our relationships, our relationship with God is healed. Forgiveness is the Holy Spirit's great teaching. Relationships become holy when their original purpose of preserving guilt is changed to forgiveness. All people drawn into our lives are part of the curriculum for undoing our guilt. When you meet someone, remember it is a holy encounter.

The people who present us with the greatest problems are the very people we should feel most grateful for. They are showing us some part of ourselves that needs healing. The Holy Spirit transforms our problems into learning opportunities. Our most upsetting relationships are giving us the greatest opportunities

Note, the Holy Spirit must be at the center of our relationships. The Holy Spirit is the only true therapist because only the Holy Spirit is conflict-free.

The path of ascension, in Markus's words:

"'Ascension buddies' is the term Sondra and I jokingly call ourselves to one another, and often we say, 'We're just little kids.' The deeper implications of these light-hearted statements place liberation and our own innocence at the center of our daily attitudes. When we married, it was a very conscious path of ascension we chose. We married in India at Babaji's ashram in the Himalayas after the nine-day Navaratri celebration spent worshiping the Divine Mother. The energy there was already very high, to say the least, and to be betrothed on this spot in front of the holy fires was very auspicious.

"Ascension is based on undoing the negative energies of our minds that keep us stuck in the lower frequencies. Obviously, anger and disapproval are lower frequencies. Feelings of insecurity and lack are also blocks to rising up. On the path of ascension, a couple must foster a spirit of gratitude in every aspect of their life. Sondra and I live a life conscious of Babaji's teachings: truth, love, simplicity, and service to humanity. We are "living into" these teachings in the sense that they are very deep and profound and require sustained attention for us to be more aware of them on a moment-to-moment basis. We can never say we have arrived because there is always a higher level, higher step in our evolution. Gratitude and forgiveness are the vehicles along the path of ascension. We cannot get impatient or desirous of something different than what *is* because what is contains the very lessons that we need to get before evolving into the next level. If there is a challenge, it is there to overcome. A challenge is there because we need it for our growth and deeper understanding to flower within us.

"Ascension is not some pie-in-the-sky idea of getting saved by some holy ghost out there in the ethers ready to sweep us up during the rapture. It is a present self-honesty that owns our results in life, unravels the causative thought factors, and accepts a clean slate in the mind where there was a bunch of toxic thoughts and memories before. There is a Holy Spirit helping you with this, but it is inside you all along. 'My Salvation come from me' is Lesson 70 in *ACIM*. You could say ascension comes from you too, from the part of you that is in communion with the sacred, the loving, the true, the simplicity of yourself. We ascend the ladder of holiness by going down into the depths of our own subconscious mind and forgiving all of those conflicts, traumas, grievances, and darkened corners that keep us attached to the past experiences of problems, death, and suffering.

"Without some time spent every day on your spiritual evolution, it is not possible to ascend. There is so much to undo—all the conditioning of our parents, family, marriages, church, educational system, social environment, workplace. All these are a challenge to our ascension process. This is why a discipline of daily spiritual practice is necessary to ascend. Read lofty books, spend time in quietude, give time to creative expression, take walks of appreciation in nature, give yourself the space to be relaxed and without any pressure from outside. Most of all, nurture a spirit of gratitude and appreciation for every moment of your life. The purpose of life is not to work at some job and be miserable in the drudgery of survival. The purpose of life is to liberate yourself from limitation, lack, sorrow, and even death. The purpose of life is to realize perfect happiness that does not make death and sorrow real. In Sonnet 146, Shakespeare describes the ascension process:

Buy terms divine in selling hours of dross;
Within be fed, without be rich no more:
So shalt thou feed on Death, that feeds on men,
And Death once dead, there's no more dying then.

"To ascend we must undo our thoughts of death and feed on them as Shakespeare pointed out. Being rich no more means that you place your internal life of the mind and spirit over your external life of acquisition and physical survival. This does not mean you disregard the body's needs and the mind's needs for refinement and beauty; but it does mean you have to overcome your attachments to limitation and death. Use the hours of work to support your inner life of the spirit. This is the proper use of your energy. Ascension is your function, and the rewards of immortality come to those who erase their limiting thoughts [of death] through forgiveness."

Overcoming the Thought: "Nothing works!"

There is one big sabotaging thought that a person could have, which could invalidate everything in this book and everything you ever learn to help yourself. That thought is this: "Nothing works." You could have that thought and not even realize it. It is also part of the unconscious death urge. If you think nothing works, then nothing will work for you. Then you will prove you are right, and you will reinforce that thought with failed attempts to change and healing, and things will only get worse and not work even more.

Let me tell you a story. I had a student who was a man, and he kept telling me that nothing works. I kept telling him that nothing works because he had the thought that nothing works. He kept telling me he knew nothing worked because that was his experience. I kept telling him thought precedes experience, but he refused to get it. One day I said to him, "You know what, I bet I am going to meet you in twenty-five years, and you are going to tell me the same thing, nothing works." I gave up trying to convince him. Guess what? I met him twenty-five years later, and so I asked him how things were going. He said to me, "Nothing works." I reminded him that I told him to give up that thought twenty-five years ago. He had not remembered it, and he was even more convinced now that nothing works after twenty-five more years of proving that to himself.

Even then he refused to get that his thought came first before his experience. So don't fall into that trap! You will only create hell for yourself. "Nothing works," like all other negative thoughts, produces its experiential proof.

Devotion and Doing Spiritual Practices Together

Participating in spiritual practices and doing devotions together cleanse our being and bring us nearer to the Holy Spirit. Here are some suggestions for devotions you can do with your partner. They will enhance your relationship and turn your whole life into one of spiritual intimacy.

Imagine the following activities as being part of your daily life as a couple. Imagine electing one or two to do together every day.

- Liberation Breathing®
- Reading *A Course in Miracles*
- Chanting
- Writing affirmations
- Meditation
- Fasting
- Being in conscious silence for long periods
- Ho'oponopono
- Praying aloud or in silence
- Fire purification
- Sweat lodges
- Attending seminars together
- Reading spiritual poetry
- Listening to spiritual music
- Networking
- Committing to a peace project

- Spending time at an ashram
- Visiting holy places
- Painting or drawing

The devotions that Markus and I do together every morning after showering and before going to the computer works for us. When we don't do them, the day does not go as well. When we do them, we are filled with energy all day, and things always go better throughout the day. In the following order we

1. do our personal mantras on mala beads (while taking a walk);
2. read the 108 Divine Mother names;
3. read out loud the names on our prayer list, people in need of support;
4. do the Ho'oponopono twelve-step process;
5. recite forgiveness prayers;
6. recite prosperity prayers;
7. read and discuss the lesson for the day from *A Course in Miracles*; and
8. play spiritual music and spend time Liberation Breathing®.

Many times we have resisted this practice, such as after Markus's father died. We only got stuck; it did not work. When we pushed through the resistance and started again, it was such a relief.

You say you don't have time? Consider getting up an hour earlier or not staying up so late to watch TV. My experience is that you end up with more time by doing these daily disciplines because you get things done more quickly. It all depends on what your priorities are. All my spiritual teachers have said that being on the path of holiness should be your top priority. It is not like joining a tennis club and playing tennis once a month. It is something that must be part of your daily life as a top priority.

Worship

To worship is to revere the worth of someone or something. In the book *Being a Christ!*, Ann and Peter Meyer (who claim to have received the book from Babaji) say the following:

"Worship is the highest, most non-judgmental form of love. If we worship a person, we see no wrong in him whatsoever. We open ourselves completely to him and become his willing servant. If we worship a teacher, we will learn very, very quickly and completely from him; for we will be open and receptive to all he has to say."

By worshipping, you will gain the most out of life. By worshipping, you will feel the best you can feel. Worship is natural; not to worship is unnatural. There are many religious ceremonies that are forms of worship. Chanting (singing mantras) and doing japa (saying prayers or mantras on mala beads) are forms of worship that do not need to take place inside a church. The highest form of prayer is gratitude—a true form of worship. Worship, however, is invalid unless we worship all of life. We need to bless the trees, the plants, the flowers, the waters, the fish, the birds, the wind, the insects, the animals, all humanity, and all life on earth and in the entire universe. These are all manifestations of the Divine Mother of Creation.

The Altar

A wonderful way to love God is to prepare one or more altars in your home. I learned this in Bali. I was stunned to see that every single home had an altar and a temple. Not only that, they use these temples daily. Each family relates to seven different temples on the island. They would not consider starting the workday without doing daily prayer rituals and making offerings. Every morning, the whole family sits together and prepares elaborate flower and fruit decorations. These preparations, along with a lot of incense, are placed on the altar along with the prayers. Then and then only do they begin their work, which is all dedicated to the divine. They actually take these offerings to their workplace where they have other altars. They do a ceremony before they put the offering on the altar at work. It is very beautiful to watch.

The Balinese were such a great inspiration for me that the first thing I did when I returned was to prepare a temple room. It was so pleasurable that, before I knew it, I had an altar in every room, even the bathroom. You might have resistance to an altar if you have not cleared your feeling about religion and any disappointment or confusion you had around that subject. When you forgive everything that was confusing and did not work and you are grateful for what did work, then you are ready. It does not matter what religion you were raised in. What matters is the reverence and love for God now. An altar will help you achieve this reverence, this respect. It will remind you to think holy thoughts and perhaps inspire you to do spiritual purification practices. It will remind you of your absolute connection to God.

I know people who are afraid of what their friends would think. My experience is that when people come to our place, they do not want to leave. They always comment on the energy, and they feel more respectful and begin thinking of their own spiritual self. We frequently burn incense in our home—two of my favorites, Amritaprasad and rose from Ammachi (my female master) or Amma's Rose available at www.amma.org.

On your altar, you can place the following:

- a beautiful altar cloth
- picture or pictures of the Master you relate to (Jesus, Virgin Mary, Babaji, Ammachi, etc.)
- candles
- flowers
- incense holder and incense
- crystals
- any personal holy objects.

Sometimes when I have a problem, I write Babaji a letter and place it under my altar cloth. I absolutely bare my soul. Here is how I write the letter:

1. Dear Babaji, my problem is this : (Only do one problem per letter)
2. The negative thoughts I had that created this problem were _____.
3. I lay these at your feet
4. My new affirmations are these _____ (opposite of number 2).

5.   Please add energy to these new thoughts.

6.   Thank you. Signed

Help and solutions come quickly this way. It has never failed. If you are really stuck and your mind needs to be snapped, try lying face down in front of your altar. This sounds a bit drastic, but it really works to show your subconscious mind you are surrendered to a higher power than just your own.

I have a great story about the incredible result of having altars in my home. I was gone from my California apartment and working in Philadelphia when I learned there was a big fire in my building. Most people lost everything and/or all their things were ruined. When I came home, the hallway leading to the apartments was black with tar, and the paintings in the hall had melted into the wall. The wreath on my door was melted into the door itself. The inside of my neighbor's place was totally covered with soot. I remember opening my door with trepidation and peering around, amazed. There was not one speck of soot anywhere! I am convinced that the altars and all my sacred art did the trick. Of course, maybe Babaji saved it!

Chanting or Doing Japa

Chanting is a type of singing that is both a form of praise and a form of purification. I will emphasize here the purification aspect of it, since the aspect of praise is more obvious. Chanting a mantra is one of the most powerful things you can do for yourself. Chanting with your mate is really great! A mantra is a sacred syllable, word, or set of words that when said and/or sung in repetition helps one attain perfection and God realization. Japa is a word used in the East to describe the act of saying the mantra repeatedly on mala beads. The 108 beads that make up the mala are moved in rhythm with the breath and the mantra to help prevent distraction.

The mantra Om Namaha Shivai is the main mantra we use because Babaji says it is actually the highest thought in the universe. It is in Sanskrit because Sanskrit is one of the oldest languages, and it is more powerful to chant in that language since it is not watered down. Its literal meaning is "Oh, Lord Shiva, I bow to thee in reverence." Shiva is that part of God that burns or destroys our ignorance and negativity. The mantra has many meanings; for example, it also means Infinite Spirit, Infinite Being, and Infinite Manifestation. Chanting it helps you manifest what you want. It also means, "Oh, Lord, you are my refuge, Thy will be done." So it can be aligned with Christianity that way. It also means "I bow to the God within," so it helps end the separation.

The mantra is like nectar nourishing you. It is like plugging yourself into the Source. It charges you up. It leads to remembering your total union with God. It is a form of spiritual intimacy that enlivens the inner consciousness and helps to overcome suffering. It provides protection and brings inner peace.

Behold the glory and the power of the divine name! The divine name, or mantra, is divinity. God's name is the greatest treasure on earth. The chanting of God's name or mantra is one of the best forms of devotion there is. Repetition of the mantra with singing or saying it purifies the heart. You can achieve all things through japa. Japa yoga is the quickest, easiest, safest, surest, and cheapest way of attaining God realization. The divine name burns out all your karma and errors. The name of God is the master key for success in life!

Even *A Course in Miracles* talks about this. "I call upon God's name and on my own" is Lesson 192, and "The name of God is my inheritance" is Lesson 193. So even Jesus is saying that calling on the name of God or reciting a holy sound in which your oneness with your Creator is activated and enhanced is a valuable practice of spiritual intimacy.

The name of God is also a cure for all disease. You can take the medicine (repeating God's name) for curing anything, and you can administer this medicine to others by sitting at the side of the patient and singing or saying the mantra. This is called divine *namapathy*. The only real doctor is God, and the real cure is accepting your oneness with God. Jesus says, "Only salvation [realization of this oneness and innocence] can be said to cure" in Lesson 150 of *ACIM*. The medicine is the mantra! Using this mantra is a very healing vibration for spiritual intimacy in the new frequency for relationships. It can be applied to anything that is not supremely joyous in your life.

CDs with the mantra in different tunes are available from the Babaji ashram in Colorado. Visit www.babajiashram.org You can also order malas there.

Meditation

Meditation cannot be done by thinking. Nor does meditation mean trying to make your mind go blank. Nor is it a kind of hypnosis or suggestibility. It has nothing to do with the occult either. Meditation might be called a sustained attention for awareness and a harnessing of our latent mental power. It might simply be a method for jumping into the unconscious. It does consist of training the mind so that you can go from the surface level of consciousness into its very depths.

But to jump there without thinking, attention is needed. This pure observation will push you to the unknown. The attention is a tool to put your rational mind at ease. Sufis used dance as the tool. Zen teachers used koans (puzzles). Rajneesh used a vigorous method called chaotic meditation with catharsis. Maharishi uses a personal mantra that you are given by an instructor. You say this mantra silently to yourself. This is called Transcendental Meditation™. You can also make up your own music meditations and study the results upon yourself.

In his book, *Practical Spirituality*, John Randolph Price defines meditation as "a relaxing of the body, a stilling of the emotions, and a narrowing of attention so that the mind may contemplate the inner reality and move into another dimension in consciousness. It is a gentle raising of vibrations so that one may come into alignment with the spiritual self."

Meditation is known to reduce high blood pressure, contribute to mental clarity, alleviate stress, increase the stability of the nervous system, increase the ability to learn, and so on. But he says that of even greater importance are the spiritual benefits, i.e., to establish a channel resulting in an outpouring of the higher energy of spirit. In other words, meditation is a form of spiritual intimacy wherein you are opening your channel of being able to receive the life energies of a much greater *life force*. You have to empty your mind of all the concepts you hold onto in order to do this. You have to be willing to admit your intellect does not *know*, but your Creator in you, the Divine Intelligence in you, does know. You have to get yourself out of the way for true meditation to take place. Then meditation become effortless and permeates everything you do. You could be doing the dishes absorbed in a meditation or writing an e-mail. Just reading this book is a meditation, an attention you are giving to develop spiritual intimacy.

Fasting

This is a wonderful purification technique to do together as a couple to get to a new vibration of spiritual intimacy.

The practice itself puts you in a different frequency and to do it together is very rewarding for your relationship. Recently, my husband and I did a seven-day fast only on water. We found the resulting clarity amazing, and we got very high together.

People usually think fasting is hard and boring. I'd like to offer you another approach. It can actually be easy and fun. I can honestly say to you, "Why deny yourself the pleasure of fasting?"

First you have to let go of all your negative thoughts and belief systems about fasting. Be willing to see this differently. Imagine that this is the first time you have heard of it. As with anything, your experience of fasting will depend upon what your thoughts about it are. If you think it will be difficult then you will probably make it difficult. You would also do well to give up the thought, "I need three meals a day to survive."

In my book, *The Only Diet There Is*, you will read about people who eat almost nothing at all. They live on the light of God. There is a lesson in *A Course in Miracles* that reads, "I am sustained by the love of God." That thought helps a lot with fasting.

Fasting is frequently recommended in the Bible. It is a good way to feel the love of God because you are purifying your body and, in doing so, can channel much more of God's love and energy. You can do everything better and with greater clarity as you get so much more energy. In my fasting experience, I have received tremendous spiritual rewards and surprises. Getting rewards and surprises in the typical sense is not the reason for fasting; rather, it is a byproduct of the purity obtained.

You can begin by fasting on juice one day a week. Then increase it to two days on occasion. For me it is actually easier to do a five-day fast because I know I am really going to go for it. The real value of fasting starts coming after the third day. This is when you start to get the supreme benefits. And if you can make it for ten days, you can be sure something will transform in you! Most people are tempted to quit after the second day. This is a shame because it is really only the first two days that can be hard. About the third day, in my experience, you tend to forget about food and begin to experience the lack of desire to eat. This is when it becomes fun and interesting.

This is all easier if you are in a special setting. If you are doing your usual work routine, fasting may require a lot more fortitude, especially if your friends keep inviting you out to eat and you go! Even this, however, can be done. I deliberately tried that once. I accepted all invitations and consumed nothing.

If you would like to read about different fasts, I recommend the book *Are you Confused?* by Dr. Paavo Airola. You could start on the master cleanse, which is made of pure water, lemon juice, maple syrup, and cayenne. I experienced no hunger at all. I also recommend reading *The Miracle of Fasting* by Paul Bragg.

I deliberately do not fast to lose weight although you can. It works, but after feeling deprived, you might stuff yourself later. That is the risk. I fast for spiritual reasons and then it feels like a reward instead of a punishment.

If you are a leader or head of a company, you will be amazed how this will affect your whole business. People are telepathic. They spontaneously start cleaning stuff up, shaping things up!

Fasting with your mate is a very, very powerful practice of spiritual intimacy.

Silence

Think of what it might be like to go into silence with your mate for an extended period of time. Some people are afraid of silence because they are afraid of their own thoughts. But once you are on the path toward enlightenment, you know you can easily change your negative thoughts to positive ones and that there is nothing to be afraid of. You are in charge of your own mind and feelings. In silence, you are not distracted so much from your own divinity. Silence provides an exquisite opportunity to remember your connection to God. The voice of the Holy Spirit can come through when you are in silence. New ideas come to you, new ways of clearing problems. You become more creative. Your body starts clearing itself. Your feelings become more sensitive. Having your mate nearby and touching him or her becomes exquisite. It is good to do this at home but perhaps even better is away from home in a beautiful spot. It is important to be away from constant distractions.

Sometimes couples even need solitude, and this quiet, centered, alone time enhances the relationship. It is a form of spiritual intimacy that you don't need to talk about! It is one of the best ways I know to be spiritually nourished. It is very different from being lonely; there is no loneliness. You come back to the relationship refreshed and clear. You can even be silent and in solitude together. We have a day in silence on the India Quest, and people feel their whole inner guidance system opening up. Take a day of silence, twenty-four hours, and at the end of that time, share with you mate your new insights and inspirations.

Prayer

A lot of people have given up on prayer, thinking it does not work because they have not received what they wanted in the past. If that is your case, I would suggest you carefully read the book *Ask and It is Given* by Esther and Jerry Hicks. When one does not receive what is asked for, there is a problem with allowing. There is often a sabotaging thought in the subconscious that has to be cleared (that is where breathwork/Liberation Breathing® comes in). Often there is too much fear and doubt about receiving what one is asking for. The *Course* says the Holy Spirit will not add to your fear.

If you have asked for a marriage and did not get it, perhaps you have too much fear of love—you are too afraid of being hurt again or whatever negative past experience you are harboring. The Holy Spirit has to wait then until you work out your fear. Or let's say you are praying for a miracle overnight for the healing of your disease. *A Course in Miracles* explains that we have a fear of miracles. Pray for release of the fear of the miracle first. Ultimately, pray for help in the resolution of the cause of your fear. So then, when your prayers are not answered, do not blame God. Only you can deprive yourself of anything. The Source is abundant and wants to give to you. The giver expands by giving. God wants you to have all the gifts of the kingdom.

The initial phase of prayer is one of emptying. Pouring out the contents of the heart (emptying the cup) without editing or embarrassment, withholding nothing, is a prerequisite. It is important to bring the mind to silence and stillness. You can do this emptying process by just observing your thoughts. You can sit quietly in a chair, close your eyes, and just watch your thoughts pass by like they are clouds passing across a blustery sky.

A method of prayer I learned as a child is very effective. It contains five parts. It is very pleasurable to do this out loud with your mate.

1. Opening
2. Forgiveness
3. Gratitude
4. Petition
5. Closing

Opening

Set the stage, create the ambiance and establish the connection. Read from the scriptures or from spiritual or metaphysical books. This would be a great time to read a few pages from the text of *ACIM*.

Forgiveness

Ask for pardon for anything you feel is your wrongdoing. Ask to be forgiven by any specific person or forgive someone you need to forgive.

Gratitude

Specifically express gratitude for the things you have—friends, love, the life you have, your good health, and so on. Remember that the law of gratitude must be acknowledged. It will also increase your good.

Petition

Now you are in the proper context to ask for help or guidance in any specific area. Talk to the Holy Spirit freely, knowing and having faith that you will receive.

Closing

This again is when you read or listen to spiritual literature or spiritual poetry. To me, this is the perfect time to do the lesson for the day in *A Course in Miracles*.

Praying is not only wonderful to do with your mate as a daily ritual; it is excellent for the whole family to do together. I have given prayers to couples who were in stress in their marriage and on the verge of divorce. They have reported to me that it saved their marriage.

Begging is a low form of prayer. The highest form of prayer is gratitude for and celebration of your connection to the Source. I refer you to *A Course in Miracles* sequel called *Song of Prayer* and will quote a few paragraphs here:

"Prayer is practice of the presence of God. A thankful mind attracts good. Try to get to the point where you are giving thanks instead of complaining, fearing, or worrying."

If you do petition, pray from the standpoint of already having what you ask for (knowing that there is no spiritual lack).

- Lay hold of the good you desire
- Recognize it is here and now
- Have absolute confidence
- Express gratitude

Babaji, our master, told us that faith is everything. When you develop a consciousness of the things you seek, they will appear in your presence. However, if your consciousness of need is greater than your consciousness of God, then need will expand. When you love God more than your problem, then you will get somewhere.

Ho'oponopono

If you have not heard of Ho'oponopono, it is my great honor and privilege to introduce you to this ancient Hawaiian clearing technique. I thank Morrnah Simeona, supreme kahuna, for giving me permission to share with you.

This technique, a combination of special Hawaiian prayers and breathing processes, is one the sweetest, most gentle, and beautiful ways I know to free and purify yourself. Ho'oponopono provides a step-by-step approach to achieving peace, balance, and a new meaning to life through an understanding of one's self-identity. It is a process which means to set right, to correct, and to rectify errors through repentance, forgiveness, and transmutation.

If you read books on the huna (secret) religion of the kahunas (keepers of the secret) or my book, *Pele's Wish*, you will find that they knew exactly what they were doing.

They could heal people instantly, change weather, set bones, affect the elements, and on occasion, resurrect the dead. I highly recommend taking a Ho'oponopono class so you can learn the technique for yourself. Look it up on the Internet at http://www. self-i-dentity-through-hooponopono.com/(Foundation of I). This is the official organization that Morrnah Simeona left in charge to teach the work. They give classes all over the world and, most likely, in your area. If you want to have some other insights into the power of Hawaiian spirituality, you can also read my book, *Pele's Wish*. It recounts many of experiences in Hawaii that made this lineage a major part of my spiritual practice. It also discusses on how to become a modern-day kahuna.

Fire Purification

Fire purification is an ancient technique for clearing one's aura and one's karma and for releasing anger, guilt, and so on. It is quite simple: all you have to do is meditate on the fire with your eyes open. This can be done with a fireplace, an open bonfire, or lacking these, with a candle. You sit quietly and look at the flame. About this technique Babaji said,

"Worshipping the fire means worshipping the inner light. Worshipping the fire burns karma. It is spiritual purification. Worshipping the fire transforms into pure love all that is impure in the heart and mind. The power of the holy fire is that the flame of love unfolds the qualities of the soul."

Indian Sweat Lodges

Always and only do a sweat lodge with a medicine man or woman who knows what he or she is doing. There have been serious mistakes made by others that have caused greater harm than good. So one should make sure you have an experienced Indian medicine man.

It is one of the great traditions of the American Indians. Usually this ritual occurs in an appropriate and beautiful outdoor wooded setting, preferably by a cold stream. The sweat itself is done in a low igloo-like tent with a fire pit in the middle. Hot rocks are brought in on a pitchfork. When the pit is filled with the rocks, the tent's flap is lowered. The medicine man, having done all of the ritualistic preparations and prayers, begins to put sacred roots on the fire. Then he begins to throw water on the rocks while chanting. Then you sweat. He chants and you sweat. You sweat, he chants. When you feel like you cannot take any more, he throws open the flap and everyone runs to the stream and immerses. The cycle is then repeated two more times. At least that is the way one excellent sweat lodge that I attended went.

The exquisite feeling of purity after a sweat is something to behold! I want to emphasize that this experience is very strong, and I would definitely recommend you do it with an American Indian medicine man or woman.

Liberation Breathing®

Doing Liberation Breathing® is magical because, for one, it is a rejuvenation process. Your body is rejuvenated with divine energy. The feeling of being automatically renewed produces tremendous joy. The deep, connected, circular breathing also increases your ability to receive love as it opens your heart. It is an ultimate spiritual intimacy you have with yourself.

Liberation Breathing® improves your relationships, especially when both partners are receiving the blessing and benefits of this deep but simple process because it frees you from the unconscious conditions that you inherited from your family. It can also help you become more creative and intuitive. This happens as you clear you ego (false self) and the sabotaging negative thoughts held in your subconscious so that you can experience the availability of infinite intelligence. It is a sacred thing really because you are connecting with the source of life itself. It is like a sacrament because you are taking in the Holy Spirit. Spiritual healing is a byproduct. Joy is the result. Who wouldn't want that?

Liberation Breathing® can release accumulated negativity back to and including birth. It is a rejuvenation process that can release tension in the body. It can liberate you from

- the trauma of birth,
- negative thoughts and patterns,
- pain and disease,
- fears of failure or fears of success,
- fears in general,
- guilt,
- anger,
- the parental disapproval syndrome,
- doubt and hesitancy,
- misery and depression,
- beliefs and programming of old age,
- the unconscious death urge, and
- stuck past lives.

Through Liberation Breathing® you will have the ultimate spiritual intimacy with your self and your Creator. It will open gateways into your heart that you had long ago closed. It will cleanse your cells of negative thought contaminations stored and crystalized in the very DNA. It will flush out the crud that will eventually accumulate in your system and kill you.

And more, Liberation Breathing® is the ultimate cosmic bath. It is for *everyone*. No matter who you are or where you are on the path, it will take you higher than you ever thought you could go. You will wonder how you ever lived without it. You are actually surrendering to the healing force of your own aliveness with a maximum of ease and a minimum of struggle and resistance.

The art of it is about letting go, releasing control, and getting your mind out of the way. The science of it is about adjusting your breath and correcting your thoughts.

The spiritual dimension of this conscious breathing is the heart of the matter. The purpose of it is not just the movement of air but the movement of energy. Because the energy is accumulating as you are not using it up by jogging, let's say, then you experience dynamic energy flows in your body. These energy flows are the merging of spirit and matter. These energy flows we describe as tingling and vibrating sensations. When these are happening, your body is being filled with pure life energy, and your mind and body are being cleansed of tension and impurities.

The conscious breathing method we are talking about was originally called rebirthing because any conscious breathing can stimulate birth memories. We are healing the damage done to the breath mechanism at birth, which resulted in most people sub-ventilating (shallow unconscious breathing). Sub-ventilation, which most people do all their lives, does not promote longevity. We are retraining the breath mechanism. It is a highly personal experience in which people often have mystical experiences. Breathwork is now practiced around the world and is very popular.

Our work has now been enhanced, and Liberation Breathing® is a new expression of it. During the last part of the session as Markus and I have been guided by the Divine Mother, we recited certain prayers and mantras which made it all even safer and deeper. I constantly hear how people's lives have changed completely due to this process.

We consider Liberation Breathing® a life-long spiritual path, the ultimate goal being ascension. Eventually, you can learn to do it on yourself. However, in the beginning, it is most important to have ten sessions with a man and ten sessions with a woman. Doing it with a man will bring up your father issues and doing it with a woman will bring up mother issues.

It is done dry and wet and privately or in a group. In the dry session, you are lying down on your back on a bed or on the floor on a mat with the Liberation Breathing® facilitator sitting next to you and guiding you.

The wet version is done in a hot tub, Jacuzzi, or bathtub, using a snorkel and nose plug to breathe as you float face down in warm water in the fetal position. There is even cold-water Liberation Breathing®, which is a lot more intense and which is very good for releasing anesthesia from birth and death energy. By death energy, I mean death programming that gets most activated after someone close to you dies. Or if a person is very depressed, that would be death energy also.

Group Liberation Breathing® or rebirthing is done in a large room where a number of people (who have been well prepared) lie down on the floor on mats and do the process together. This is best done during seminars. In our case, we do a breathing session at the end of the day in every seminar no matter what the topic is. This helps people integrate the data and release emotional reactions. One should continue with dry sessions until one has worked out the bulk of one's birth trauma. Then you begin wet sessions and eventually when your guide says you are ready, you can learn to do it on yourself. For more on this, e-mail Markus Ray at manmohan1008@gmail.com.

Imagine installing a wonderful Jacuzzi or hot tub in your bedroom, living room, or outside. As a daily routine, a couple (or even the whole family) soaks together and rebirths each other instead of arguing. During the session, they let go of tension, pain, and disease-producing stress. They channel new ideas for their business, relationship, or future. They get clear on their relationship problems. Does this scenario sound farfetched? It isn't. There are thousands of breathworkers already living like this right now.

"But, Sondra, I am not a trained breathworker," you say. Well, yes, you should not try unless you are. But we can teach you and easily. Imagine the fun of having other friends come over and sharing the experience with you as an alternative to watching TV! Imagine helping each other openly with problems we all experience. The breathwork community is supportive. We get high together on love and air. You can too. It is becoming a way of life in many places.

Liberation Breathing® is not therapy. It is a gentle form of spiritual purification in which you are honest with yourself and your Creator. Regarding analysis, the *Course* says, "How can you get the light by analyzing the darkness?" This is an important statement to ponder. Liberation Breathing® is pouring in more light, more forgiveness, more acceptance and love into your system, not to mention more prana and life energy than you have ever been used to. And you are not burning up the energy like when you are exercising or jogging. So the added energy has an innate intelligence to go to the areas in your mind and body most in need of healing. You breathe in more love while you release stored-up fear. And the results are almost always miraculous.

At the beginning of this relationship, we recommend that each person has a breathwork/Liberation Breathing® session by a skilled facilitator outside of the relationship. Only after they work through the majority of the birth trauma and unconscious death urge should they consider facilitating for each other. Later, you can get trained how to rebirth each other and yourself. Liberation breathing can save your life and your relationships. If that were not so, I would not have dropped everything and dedicated my whole life to the teaching of it.

Imagine this scene: You are tired, cranky; you have a migraine. You don't even want to see your mate. You just cannot be bothered. You feel overwhelmed by the kids. You want to give up. Your mate gets angry, and it gets worse. It takes a week to recover from the upset. That is the old paradigm. Now imagine this: You feel a headache coming on. You tell your mate you need to go into the breathing room or hot tub. Your mate comes and assists you. You discover the thoughts you have that are causing this potential migraine. You breathe them out. You feel fantastic after only twenty minutes. If this sounds like an appealing alternative to your current circumstances, why not join us for an easier life? Contact us via www.liberationbreathing.com and read more about our work around the world at www.liberationbreathing.blogspot.com.

Devotion in Markus's words:

"The broad spectrum of devotional practices that Sondra mentions above can be summed up in one word: attention. What you give your attention to is what you are devoted to, and what you could say you worship. You could be devoted to classical music, to art, to nature, to baseball for that matter. You could be devoted to writing novels or books on relationships. When your attention to something is so passionate and whole, you love it above all else and you cannot wait to devote your time and effort to it, then you are entering the realm of spiritual intimacy. It could be something you are doing to be productive and earn money. You love the work so much, it becomes worship. You have spiritual intimacy with your work so much so, you can hardly believe people are willing to pay you to do it. You take it seriously, and it is a form of service to others. They receive joy and happiness from you because you have put your soul and heart into what you do, and they can feel it. It is something beautiful you have done for God, for yourself, and for them. It brings meaning to your life, and you are happy as well. The happiness you feel is contagious. People want to be around that energy of joy and celebration you put into what you do. Then your life becomes a blessing to yourself and others. It is what I mentioned my teacher Tara Singh referred to as the art of living. When you are fully attentive to what you love, your life is one of devotion. Your daily actions become a dance in the ballet of appreciation. Your words become music in the expression of joy and gladness. You find yourself more and more in a state of spiritual intimacy.

"Devotion enables you to better dissolve problems. This problem at work, that problem in relationships, a problem in school or a problem with health, our life seems racked with problems. What would solve these problems? What would give us the space to devote to something else, to our happiness, to our spiritual life, to our liberation from problems? Spiritual intimacy is the solver of all problems.

"Again I received the most wise solution from my teacher Tara Singh. He imparted to me an attention to stillness and silence. In the spaciousness inside myself, there is a place where all problems are solved. It does not require managing and figuring out solutions; rather, it requires the relinquishment of trying to figure things out.

He related this story to me. Someone asked the Buddha how he solved a problem. The Buddha replied, "I never get into one." Obviously stillness and silence do not make problems. The Buddha had brought his mind to a state of stillness and silence, which is the nature of the Source, and he had no more need for problems. The Buddha was in a state of spiritual intimacy all of the time. Spiritual intimacy does not make any problem real; therefore, it never gets into one.

"All of the practices of spiritual intimacy are meant to bring us to this place of inner peace. The whole of *A Course in Miracles* is to bring us to a state of mind in which there are no problems. The wise would free us from problems in every instance because they see that all problems are self- projected. If we really saw that all of our problems we made up, would we keep making them up? Attention to that state of mind of stillness and silence, to spiritual intimacy is something that you must give to yourself in the moment, every moment. It is not something you can cultivate through a rigid formula or system, but it does require sustained attention or practice. You have to be determined to have a relationship with spiritual intimacy itself above all else. As Sondra said mentioned above, 'How can you get the light when you are analyzing the darkness?' Analyzing the problem never solves the problem; it just shifts around the focus. Dr. Wayne Dyer wrote, 'There is a spiritual solution to every problem.' The solution comes from a deep abiding intimacy you have between your self and your source.

"Lesson 80 in *ACIM* says, 'Let me recognize the problem has been solved.' It says the only problem is separation from your source and the Source's will for you is only happiness. So there are no problems in life that are real. They are all mental projections of this one problem of separation, which the *Course* goes on to say are not real because separation is impossible. You cannot be separated from the source of life, obviously or you would not be here reading this. Awareness of this divine connection with your source free of all problems is spiritual intimacy.

"Well, you are going to say, a flood just swept through Nashville and destroyed my house. That is not a mental projection. That could be true, but how attached are you to your material possessions? What is your relationship to life itself? Are you grateful for your own life? (Some people died in the flood). Are you grateful to be alive for another day? For the people who came forward to help you? For the many rich experiences that life has already brought? In the face of disaster there is some other action that is taking place. Perhaps you are better served with a different set of circumstances, and life is moving you into them. Perhaps you are being pressed to discover your hidden potentials. When you see the action of life with an element of stillness and silence, problems become adventures and opportunities for growth.

"I go on to say, 'Leaving my marriage put me in a new frequency. My new life became one of gratitude and appreciation instantly. And my old life became one of gratitude and appreciation as well through forgiveness for my mistakes.' I was stepping into the unknown, but my devotion to Sondra and our relationship of real spiritual intimacy was worth more to me than battling it out with my former wife about who was going to walk away with more of the divisible assets. I had to deal with some internal fears of having nothing from what I had spent thirty years accumulating, but it was a freedom I had never felt before. I stepped into a new devotion and new attention to that place of stillness and silence within myself that did not get into problems. I was free to devote myself totally to my liberation, to my salvation, to my total happiness. Essentially, I devoted myself to a life of spiritual intimacy.

"Devotion is to your self. People have been searching all of their lives for just this. When all of your external dreams are gone, you will be left with the stillness and silence within that is more valuable than any pursuits. Your seeking has come to an end, and you are devoted to the peace of God. You want that more than anything else, and you do not have to go anywhere or do anything to find it. It surrounds you constantly with its care and envelops you in all you do. Through devotional practice, your communion with your Creator is an action of spiritual intimacy that gives your life its ultimate pure joy and meaning."

14

A Marriage in the New Frequency of Spiritual Intimacy

If I ask my single friends how they feel about marriage, they usually say, "Why should I get married when nearly all of my married friends are unhappy in marriage or getting divorced?" Well, yes, if they are in the old paradigm that probably is so. Marriage can accentuate all human problems. It cannot be based on limited motives such as sex or financial gain since it would most likely rapidly deteriorate into selfishness. But behind the words of my friends, I hear a secret wish that they could somehow have the dream of a marriage that would be the safe haven or refuge they imagined. They wish for a new kind of partnership that could actually work.

In Gary Zukav's *Seat of the Soul*, he points out how easy it is for souls who marry to fall into the orbit of the old, no-longer-functional archetype of marriage. It is obvious that souls have to create a new archetype and reinterpret marriage. He recommends making it a sacred commitment to assist in each other's spiritual growth as I have mentioned earlier.

If you are married and would like your marriage to change, you do not necessarily have to separate or get divorced to force a change, but you both probably need to invest a lot more of yourself in a spiritual process to discover the path of transformation. You have to be committed, in short, to spiritual intimacy.

The spiritual master Meher Baba said, "Marriage has to be undertaken (by both parties) as a real spiritual adventure for exploring the higher possibilities of the Spirit." From that space, you, as two enlightened souls, can offer your united love and service to humanity.

What you do with marriage determines whether it is bondage or liberation. Obviously, the goal should be to become more liberated within the structure that marriage offers. Ask yourself this question, "Am I more in the ego's thought system with my marriage or am I more in the Holy Spirit's thought system?" If you consider yourself trapped by the ego, it is time to consider a whole new model.

There was a guru named Rajneesh (Osho) who declared that marriage is out of date and that it destroys all possibilities for happiness. He insisted that marriage makes everyone a zoo animal, that it exacerbates the will to die and leads to prostitution! He believed that marriage is an anachronistic barrier that must disappear and that it has ruined the status of women!

I found this in the book *A New Vision of Women's Liberation* by Osho. Those are the most radical statements on marriage that I have read. To balance out that extreme position, I read Swami Kruyananda's book *How to Spiritualize Your Marriage*. This book advocated marriage for a number of reasons. Marriage becomes a sacred bond only if it is made sacred; otherwise, it is simply a social contract. Swami Kruyananda said the following:

- Marriage can help a person achieve inner balance (especially between reason and feeling).
- Marriage helps break the confines of selfishness and ego, helping one to learn to live in a larger reality than one's own.
- Marriage helps one expand one's identity.
- It provides a proving ground for one's inner spiritual development. It tests a married mate's spiritual qualities.
- Marriage is a vehicle through which one can achieve union with God (after achieving union with the God in your mate).

Master Yogananda stated, "The desire for marriage is universal because of the cosmic power of love to draw everything back to oneness." He stressed how important it is that marriage be based on divine friendship between equals with unconditional love, unconditional loyalty, and the divine qualities of kindness, respect, trust and faith."

It became evident to me that marriage itself is not at fault; rather, it is what we do with marriage that determines whether liberation or delusion is achieved.

When you ask if you are into the ego's thought system with marriage (delusion) or into the Holy Spirit's thought system with marriage (the latter being the true reality), you are also asking, "Is this a holy relationship or an unholy relationship?" Let's review the difference.

EGO'S THOUGHT SYSTEM	HOLY SPIRIT'S THOUGHT SYSTEM
Separation	Unity/oneness
Guilt	Innocence
Fear	Love
Conflict	Peace and harmony
Pain	Relaxation
Anger	Forgiveness
Worry	Faith
Misery	Happiness and Joy
Sickness	Abundance
Depression	Perfect health
Death	More life

UNHOLY RELATIONSHIP	HOLY RELATIONSHIP
The ego's mind contracts into limited state of self-enclosure	The Holy Spirit's Mind expands into greater realms
Asks: What can I gain from the other?	Asks: What can I give?
Reinforces your case (negativity)	Purified through spiritual discipline
Causes clinging, fear, dependency	Causes trust and freedom
Sees the body as sex object	Sees body as temple to God

In an ego-based marriage, Rajneesh's analysis could be true. But if the married couple embraces the Holy Spirit's thought system, they can have a whole different picture.

My first marriage when I was young was definitely in the ego's thought system. *A Course in Miracles* did not even exist back then, and I had no guidelines. The marriage that I am now in with Markus is a whole different ball of wax. We have dedicated it to *ACIM* and agreed in the beginning that it would be without conflict. We have dedicated it to spiritual intimacy.

Marriage in the new frequency of spiritual intimacy according to Markus:

"The doorway into the new frequency of my marriage with Sondra was formed long ago, but I was not ready to walk through it. I had many life lessons I needed to learn to prepare myself for our union. The biggest lesson for me was to be absolutely clear I would commit myself to a relationship of no conflict. I learned this lesson the hard way, by being in a long relationship that was fraught with conflict that made us both miserable. I decided there must be a better way to live, to have peace and joy as a way of life. Another lesson I needed to learn was that material accumulation did not necessarily bring satisfaction. Each step on the road to more stuff seemed accompanied by a higher price to pay that asked for more and more of my energies. I felt like the man in the circus, spinning dozens of plates on sticks. I had to scramble to keep them all spinning, and at any moment, those could all come crashing down. Also, the lesson of work as divine worship had to be learned. I was an artist and a small contractor. When I no longer saw the contracting as less than the art, and I brought the art of gratitude into all that I did, work became worship. Then the biggest lesson I needed to learn was that my life needed to radically change, and I was the only one who could take responsibility for it. This change could not be determined by what anybody else thought of the change.

"When these lessons were learned I bumped into Sondra Ray again in Philadelphia after not seeing her for nearly twenty years. The rest is history. We came together as two twin flames and our meeting was fun, inspiring, and effortless. Tara Singh had prepared me for a holy relationship, one in which the evolution of our souls and realization of self Identity was a top priority. I already had a lot of reverence for Sondra and her work. As she found out more about me, her reverence for our relationship became equally powerful. Then we saw there was a destiny bringing us together, as if the Forces of Life had a plan for us beyond anything we could have dreamed up on our own. Instantly all of my life became clear and the reasons for all of my past spread out like a beautiful tapestry of divine purpose.

"We met up again in Asheville, North Carolina, for a series of Sondra's events. On Valentine's Day, Babaji's samadhi day, when he took conscious departure, Sondra asked me to come to Nashville with her. During a rebirth, my doubts dissipated, and I said yes. Within the week, I had proposed to her in Nashville in the Unity Church where she was giving a Divine Mother workshop. It was a certainty we both had that the masters had brought us together to bless our union. We were to travel to India in about a month, and we set the date of our marriage one year later in India at the Navaratri in Herakahn, the home of our master Babaji.

"In essence, the marriages we had in the old paradigm in churches too often ended up being rituals that fulfilled family expectations and traditions for only a few days. One would think that Jesus oversees a lot of marriages. But the couple has to nurture and value this relationship with the Christ on a sustained basis for the blessing to hold fast and be total. Spiritual intimacy could bring divine inspiration that sustains a new frequency for the marriage, but often, the marriage falls into an empty ritual that appeals to the family traditions and follows the options of personal agendas and social conformity. Seldom does the marriage represent a total surrender of the couple to the Heart of the Master, which is their own real heart, by the way, and to a discovery of their Divine Purpose. Therefore their bond does not grow, strengthen and flower into something creative and unique. It falls into the repetition of the mores and problems of the generations before. It stays stuck in the old paradigm of specialness, expectations, and unfulfilled desires. and memories of ever returning death.

"Sondra and I were determined not to be run by the past and just replay the old memories of our families in our marriage. We were determined to take the high road of spiritual intimacy. We were committed to ascend this road of holiness together, not descend. We were both at the same level of intensity that could ignite the fire within to live a truly God-given life. We were dedicated to holy relationship that *A Course in Miracles* speaks so much about. But we did not just want to study such lofty guidelines as an intellectual exercise; we were determined to walk the walk and live the talk.

"When we said to each other we were committed to a conflict-free relationship, we really meant it. So that means conflict is never justified. We knew we would have to value peace above all else to stay in the vibration of spiritual intimacy. We would have to practice the teachings of conflict resolution we give in the LRT® and not go to bed with any withholds of anger or resentment. Without the spiritual practices we do every day this would not be possible to sustain. Doing Liberation Breathing®, having quietude together every day, reading the lesson in *ACIM* every day, listening to beautiful and uplifting spiritual music every day keeps our life on track. And in the times of our productive work, we are certain that building good relationships locally and globally, teaching others the principles of good relationships, writing about these principles unfolding in us has made our marriage one in new frequency of divine service. All of these things I mentioned create a strong spiritual intimacy between us.

"The author Henry David Thoreau said something like, 'The greatest service any man can do for his fellow men is to rise to the height of his own being.' Tara Singh exemplified this to me; Babaji exemplified this to Sondra. And we came together with the deep gratitude that our teachers had awakened—something dynamic and powerful within us, something of our own divine nature, our own self-identity through the intensification of spiritual intimacy.

"Marriage in the new frequency is when two people, who value their own purity of being more than anything else, join. They are pure and innocent and whole by themselves. In joining, their power is doubled by bringing their twin flames together into one flame. They share that purity and innocence of light with each other and then to the world. The hand of the master is upon their heads, and they bow to the forces of life that put them together."

Markus writes about aligning with a master at our wedding:

"Our wedding in India was something far beyond the conventions of marriage in the US. Because we felt the Maha Avatar Babaji had 'arranged' our being together, we wanted to honor our marriage at the Divine Mother festival at his ashram in Herakahn. Sondra had been taking groups of Westerners to India for over thirty years. It had become her spiritual first home. Naturally, this seemed a fitting start to our new frequency for relationship. The Divine Mother festival was a powerful preparation. Each of the nine days we would participate in the ancient fire ceremony to pay homage to the supreme life force of the universe. Babaji himself had said that one day spent at the Navaratri is equal to twelve years of spiritual progress in the worldly setting. On the last day of the nine-day festival, we got married around the fire and amidst the elements. We walked seven times around the flames, made our offerings, fed each other, consecrated food, honored each other with strings of mala beads, and received the blessings of our spiritual master. We had no documents to confirm this marriage. Our teacher Muniraj had said, 'Where truth is spoken, no papers are necessary.' That affirmation was enough for us as we considered ourselves to be twin flames anyway.

"In Herakahn, we were engulfed by the high frequency of Sri Babaji. His immortal energy permeates everything, especially in his ashrams in India and around the world. As a poet, I stayed open to making contact with it. Many poems emerged out of this energy of stillness. We became joined in this essential energy we shared. I discovered a spiritual intimacy with Babaji that inspired me to write songs from my soul. I would always find the right words when I was in that quiet state of inner listening.

"Herakahn is like no other place on earth. Many congregate there from around the world—from Italy, France, Australia, Russia, USA, England, Sweden, and many other countries—to participate in the Divine Mother festival and to be in Babaji's forcefield. His presence pervades the natural beauty of the ashram, built on the mountainside above a tributary of the Ganges River, making a lasting impression on anyone who has been there. When we go, Sondra and I meditate in the cave where he manifested his body out of thin air in 1970. I wrote about our meditation experience in this poem:

In the Cave of Your Love

In the cave of Your Love, the sacred place
You manifested Your body out of thin air,
I reverse myself, and divest my mind of thought.
Not from the womb of a woman, but rather the
Divine Mother Herself sent You into form. Now
I am within the same stonewalls which contained You
in that radiant blast of Shakti that gave You
a body I could see. I am happy to feel Your
presence still, in this cave of all caves, in this
place of Your earthly origins. Kneeling low and
crawling like a babe myself, I enter the most
inner sanctum of Your physical being. It is
darker than dark, and I lose my bearings in a
short span of time and space. My mind enters another
realm, altered from its usual concern with my
thoughts and sensations. For a short while I wonder
where I am in this blackened corner of the universe,
in the bowels of the earth, apart from all I have
ever known. I leave myself behind and forget who
I am, that self I made to replace my real Identity.
But soon You come to me and fill my mind with Silence.
I bask in the expansive space of Your Love which
has no bounds. A wave of gratitude comes over me.
What good deeds did I do to merit this gift? I am
surrounded by the emptiness of stillness. This
privilege You bestow on me is from Your Grace alone.
I could not have conceived of such a gift. I am
truly blessed forever by the presence of
Your light in this cave of complete illumination.

"In the new frequency for relationships, it helps for both parties to be aligned with a spiritual master. If you are not so prone to India, there is *A Course in Miracles* as mentioned, that came directly from Jesus. It was scribed in English, and now it is translated into many languages. Essentially, it is a conversation between Jesus and you. Whoever reads it feels he is getting the instructions of the Christ directly. No longer is a church or a middleman needed for you to have a relationship with your higher self. In *ACIM*, Jesus lays out what you need to do to make this contact.

"Lesson 101 of *A Course in Miracles* states, "God's will for me is perfect happiness." For the most part, we experience happiness intermittently, and it is not perfect. Our happiness can turn into sorrow, and the joys we have had are sandwiched between our experiences of struggle and strife. We seem constantly in the pursuit of happiness. We are seeking perfect happiness, but have we ever found it? What would it take for people to realize perfect happiness? The new frequency is a state of being in perfect happiness. But you probably will not get into it without the spiritual intimacy provided by a master. They help you to go all the way.

"All the way means taking 100 percent responsibility for all events in our life. You are no longer a victim of anything, and there are no circumstances beyond your control. If something bad happens to me, there is a memory in my subconscious mind attracting this similar event. It is recurring for the purpose of me taking total responsibility for its making. Until I take this 100 percent responsibility, I cannot really invoke the forces of true forgiveness to clean this out of my consciousness. It could happen again. It takes a spiritual master to wake us up to this depth of self-honesty. They can do it because they have already done it in themselves. They are no longer deceived by the illusions of conditioned thought.

"The new frequency for relationships requires we step totally out of the temptation to blame the external for our woes. We are the deciders of our joy or our sorrow. Our thoughts precede all experience. And our divine Creator precedes all of our thoughts. Our creation is a product of God's thought. *A Course in Miracles* says, 'You are a Thought in the Mind of God.' That is a pretty lofty statement, and without a relationship with a true spiritual master, the true teacher, it would be almost impossible to realize that truth. We need them to help us undo our ignorance that we do not even know we have. One of my masters said, 'People do not even know they don't know.' In other words, their ego of knowing still runs them, and they will not get the higher truth without first seeing what they know cannot get them there. They substitute learned spiritual techniques for the space of spiritual surrender.

"Forgiveness is the real way out, but it meets with a lot of resistance. It is a way of surrendering to the fact that all pain, and even death, is self-inflicted. It is a way of taking 100 percent responsibility for all that happens to us. It is the cornerstone of the new frequency for relationships, and a means for mental and spiritual purification. Yet while you are letting go of the old and moving through the deep cleansing, it helps to be aligned with the spiritual masters who can aid you in this process toward liberation. They are the ones who help the most in the development of spiritual intimacy. Sometimes it is shocking to the system to let go of a deep-seated pattern. You need contact with the forgiveness, compassion, and commitment of the master. He or she is the one human being who is totally interested in the evolution of your soul, and they will not stop pouring their love and help into you until you reach their level in a complete holy relationship of divine communion. They are the ones with whom it is most conducive to have spiritual intimacy. Once this intimacy has been established, it is easier then to transfer this level of spiritual intimacy on to your mate."

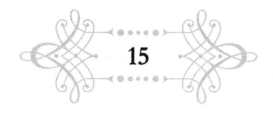

15

Children in the New Frequency of Spiritual Intimacy

Enlightened couples know that children are old souls in little bodies, and they treat them with that respect. They also know children who have been born in recent years could, in fact, have a much higher frequency than the parents themselves.

Seeing your child as your guru may be a shocking concept at first, but consider this: children are three-dimensional projections of your unconscious mind. Children act out your subconscious mind and reflect it back to you. This may drive you nuts, but if you understand this dynamics, it will improve your relationship with your children to no end. Instead of punishing them, consider instead the alternative of asking yourself what your child is trying to reflect back to you when there is a problem. What you suppress, your children will express.

Your child, like your mate, is your guru (your teacher). The principle in metaphysics goes like this: love takes upon itself your negatives, so you can see them more clearly. Your child, out of love, may take on what you are suppressing and show it to you so you can be healed of it. Listen to your children carefully.

You probably know about the work of John Bradshaw. He suggests that the best way to be a parent is to heal our own wounds from our own childhood. Your own children will give you the opportunity to do that. As your child goes through his or her developmental stages, your own wounded issues will come up at each stage.

Enlightened couples who are planning to start a family usually want to have what we call a conscious conception, a conscious pregnancy, and a conscious delivery. Each is designed to reduce birth trauma. Enlightened couples are aware that a child is not a blank slate at birth.

In our community, even young children get rebirthed. I knew a couple who were both rebirthers, and their five-year-old would grab a snorkel and nose plug and go rebirth herself in the bathtub with hot water whenever she felt stressed! Her psychic and intuitive abilities were highly developed as a result. Teach your children early that their thoughts are going to produce their results.

Recently we were in Columbia, South America, doing a lot of private counseling sessions. A father would come then the mother would come and then the teenagers would come one by one. What really blew me away was then the whole family would want to come together after that. They all came for help, and before I knew it, Markus and I were counseling whole families of four or more. It was just amazing. They all shared and took responsibility for their part. (After all, they had been in our seminars, and they knew they could not get by with being a victim.) Markus and I would ask each family member what they thought was the solution for the issues in the family. I was stunned at how accurately the teens had assessed the situation and what keen suggestions they had.

Markus's thoughts on relating to children in the new frequency:

"I did not have my own children in this lifetime. Even so, I had opportunities to relate to children and see what worked and did not work. After graduating from the Cleveland Institute of Art, I took a position next door at the Cleveland Museum of Art, teaching art in the galleries to children ages eight–twelve. The museum was very trusting and open to having these classes for the youth of the community. Often we would be conducting the classes in the galleries that contained priceless masterpieces, and the children were allowed to make their art projects with paints, crayons, paper, glue, and other potentially messy materials in front of Rembrandt's, Caravaggio's, and Ruben's paintings as though it was no big deal.

"At the time, I did not know I was relating to the children in the new frequency, but I was. The boys and girls were very alive and excited to be in the museum. Just the spaciousness of the galleries felt like being in a palace. I got to know the places in the building that were more suitable for us, spreading our projects without distracting the other visitors. We would travel around the museum, looking at various art objects from a child's perspective. They loved the colors and the shapes. The life-sized equestrian statues—the large horse with a man towering over them—were impressive. The boys liked the armor collection. The girls were very drawn to the French impressionists and Renoir's mothers with children. It was a joyous troupe through a palace of sensational delights. Art puts us in the vibe of spiritual intimacy even if we are no so aware that is what it is doing. All the much better if we are aware.

"When the time came to do their own projects of drawing, painting, or collage making, they were delighted with the sense of freedom they had to express themselves. After just a few simple guidelines and getting them set up with their materials, I would turn them loose to do whatever they wanted. They would have a blast, and so would I, watching them have a blast all under the watchful eyes of the priceless masterpieces of the Cleveland Museum of Art. Art, in this case, was fulfilling its function to lift the children and me into higher states of inner peace and joy. The children could hardly wait to run to their parents and show them their own masterpieces they made in the galleries. It was a joyous time for me, working with the children.

"When I met Tara Singh, more wisdom was imparted to me in relationship to children. He wrote two definitive books on child rearing that every parent who is serious would benefit from reading *How to Raise a Child of God* and *Awakening: A Child from Within*. Basically the parent has to come to their own inner awakening in order to impart the peace and joy of life to the child. How can a parent impart a virtuous life to their children if they themselves do not live virtuously? It is the inner wisdom of stillness and a state of nonreaction from the parent that can give the child space to be him or herself. Children are the inheritors of the inner life of the parents.

Tara Singh described the difference between education from a Western perspective and that of an Eastern perspective. In the West, we taught the accumulation of skills: how to do this and that, reading, writing, arithmetic, and engineering, economics, medicine, etc. In ancient times, the emphasis in schools of the Eastern culture was different. Lessons began by asking questions: What are the inner qualities of the person? Have the students overcome the internal impurities of anger, greed, pride, lust, and attachment? Do they have reverence for their parents, for their teacher, for God? What are their tendencies that need to be discovered and overcome? Do they have a sense of joy and gratitude? Are they naturally helpful? This is a different approach to education than teaching skills.

"You may say that skills are needed in this day and age to live in the world. That is so. The child needs to learn to be productive in something he likes to do. But the pressures of competition and acquiring skills and acquisitions can be detrimental to the child. These may put insecurity and fear into his mind. But there is another way to relate to a child in the New Frequency, which is one of Spiritual Intimacy. It starts and ends with giving them the space to just be themselves, and to evolve naturally without any pressure or parental disapproval. What would you teach your child beyond what you know? Who would teach the child not only to look, but to see that which is beyond appearance?

'I can sympathize with parents when they are caught in the artificiality of life. Our parents didn't bring us up right either; we have inherited false values. But let us not desecrate the child's mind with a repeat of our own experiences. The child brings with him the space for his own growth. Better not to crowd him with our stress and pressure. Give the child the space and you will be consistent with the Law—the Law that never intrudes on what is of God. Would you learn of simplicity? Would you learn to relate the child with his simplicity?

'The parents, and then the teachers, are the custodians of the child of God. Our responsibility is to awaken his divine faculties as well as our own. If this is not done, then we confine the child to our experience and make him time-bound.' (Tara Singh, *How to Raise a Child of God*, [Life Action Press, 1987], 153)

"To come to a stillness and peace within creates a different vibration in your relationships with children, you become more open to allow them to explore their natural inclinations. They sense you are giving them this freedom, and they respect you for it. Rather than always intervening with a lot of dos and don'ts, you give them the space to make their own decisions, you impart to them a sense of self-worth and unlimited possibilities, and their perfection is acknowledged at every stage of their growth. You give them the space to make their own discoveries about themselves, making sure it is their interest and not just something you want them to do.

"Children are our teachers in the new frequency. But we have to allow them the environment and opportunity to explore their interests and be free of pressure and expectation from the outside. The Sudbury Valley School in Massachusetts upholds this educational philosophy.

"Sudbury Valley School is a place where people decide for themselves how to spend their days. Here, students of all ages determine what they will do, as well as when, how, and where they will do it. This freedom is at the heart of the school; it belongs to the students as their right, not to be violated.

"The fundamental premises of the school are simple: that all people are curious by nature; that the most efficient, long-lasting, and profound learning takes place when started and pursued by the learner; that all people are creative if they are allowed to develop their unique talents; that age-mixing among students promotes growth in all members of the group; and that freedom is essential to the development of personal responsibility.

"'This is a radical shift from the conventional model of education in which the teacher knows best of what the child should and can have in his curriculum. In this model in the new frequency, the teacher is the process, and the more experienced adult stands by to offer his knowledge and expertise to the less experienced child, but it is the student who initiates the process. Teacher and student are on more equal footing, and the student comes forth with his innate and natural abilities to learn what interests and inspires him. It requires a much deeper connection between the teacher and the student, one that approaches spiritual intimacy that transcends just drilling in skills. It requires that the heart center of both parties be open to receive the new and truly creative."

16

Releasing Your Relationships Issues

Releasing your relationships issues to a master or a higher power makes everything easy, but *A Course in Miracles* says we probably won't do it because it is too easy. It seems we are addicted to having it hard and to struggling. But it is never too late to give up the struggle pattern.

I can vouch for the fact that this absolutely works. I want to remind you again that you can do something simple like write a letter to your master and put it under the altar cloth on your altar. You could write "Dear Jesus," "Dear Babaji," "Dear Ammachi," or simply "Dear Holy Spirit or God."

In my opinion, the letter should be a responsible letter and contain such thoughts as these:

1. This is my problem_____
2. These are the negative thoughts that caused this problem
3. I lay them at your feet (I confess having them)
4. These are my new affirmations (opposite of what comes up in number 2)
5. Please add energy to my new thoughts
6. Thank you (sign your name)

If you are not in an intimate relationship, this is a perfect communication between you and a higher power. If you are in an intimate relationship, you can say, "This is our problem..." Imagine when you both did it!

If you do not have a master or cannot relate to the word God, there is still a way to communicate to something higher. In her book *How to Make Your Relationship Work*, Anne Geraghty suggests the following method:

> "You speak to the body of the relationship which is love as a third force. You are then speaking to the body of your love. You can put that out in a chair in front of you both and talk to it. The body of your love is greater than the sum of its parts. It is greater than anger, fear, pain, betrayal, and guilt. The force will direct you if you lay everything you think and feel at the feet of the body of the relationship." (p. 26)

An example was given of one partner having a problem with smoking. The author says you sit on the side of the table, looking at the smoking issue as a problem the couple is both faced with and both would be needed to solve it.

If you have a master, it is good for both people in the relationship to join in divine intent and invoke the I Am presence (higher self) and invoke the presence of their master and ask them to work with you. You should join hands, invite in your I Am presence to overlight you both, and ask for the master you are most aligned with to join you. A group body has now been created. This takes no time at all, but how many couples will do it? One has to ask, "Do I want spiritual evolution and spiritual harmony within this group body, or do I want to remain self-centered?" This practice establishes more spiritual intimacy between a higher power, you, your mate, the problem and the solution. All are brought together for the one answer, which is always liberation from the problem.

The Importance of Each Partner Being Enlightened

In David Hawkins's book *Power vs. Force: The Hidden Determinants of Human Behavior*, he discusses levels of enlightenment.

An archangel or avatar represents a score of 1,000. An enlightened person would be 600. Someone having unconditional love would be 500, and so on.

He confirms these levels with extensive testing using kinesiology. The problem, he says, is that 78 percent of people are only at a score of 200! That is barely integrity.

He says you were born with a score, and people only go up a mere five points after birth in one lifetime. You were born with a score based on your levels of enlightenment gained in your past lives. Most people don't even think of this so that is why they go up so few points per lifetime. But what if you and your partner were consciously working on enlightenment together? The chances of raising your scores would be so much greater. And why do you want this? Because you get more happiness as your score goes up. You get more peace. You get more health and abundance.

But if one of you is not willing to work on himself or herself, what will happen? I usually see the one who is willing to do the work move on as it gets too uncomfortable to live with someone who is not.

The Immense Joy of Living with a Breathworker

I would like to impart how great it is to have two rebirthers or breathworkers living together. To me this is a miracle to behold. Why? Precisely because you can help each other clear anything through the breath.

Let's say an issue comes up that is upsetting. Instead of blaming someone else for the issue, the one who is upset should be looking at how he or she attracted the situation. But maybe they just are not ready to do that; the upset is too disturbing in the body. If his or her partner is a breathworker, the disturbed partner can approach his or her mate and say, "I really need to breathe now. Can you facilitate that?" A good breathworker will always stop what they are doing, if possible, and support their partner to breathe for an hour. The breathworker will help the partner determine how the situation was created and what lesson is to be learned from it. The partner who is upset will simply breathe out the fear, guilt, shame, or anger involved. Within an hour, the energy will have completely changed. It is really a miracle. If no action is taken to do a spiritual purification technique like breathwork, the pain remains suppressed, covered up with alcohol or drugs or some other addiction. Or the partner may take it out on the mate. That is the old paradigm, the old frequency. If neither partner is a breathworker, then hopefully, they know one they can call. But I am here to tell you that the ideal scene would be if both took a Liberation Breathing school and learned how to support each other. It keeps the relationship fresh and alive, and you feel fully supported by your partner. You feel safe knowing you have a haven right there in your own home.

17

Money in the New Frequency of Spiritual Intimacy

All metaphysical teachings on money say the same thing, and that is wealth is a state of consciousness, and you are at cause of receiving. Thinking is the key to bringing to you everything you want. The law of attraction is always in operation. You either have success thoughts or failure thoughts. Money follows your thoughts. You either have a prosperity consciousness or a poverty consciousness.

Then you must connect thought with personal action. There is a very important thing called efficient action. It goes like this. Make every small act a success. Every inefficient act is a small failure. See everything through to completion. Do every little thing well and that becomes cumulative.

What were the dynamics around money in your family? If you are a conformist, you might be unconsciously copying your parents' relationship to money. More than likely you could be stuck under the financial ceiling of your parents. If your parents were prosperous and taught you very good habits around money, be sure to have gratitude for them. It is important to look at these dynamics.

What are your religious views around money? The old idea is that poverty and sacrifice are pleasing to God. But there is nothing inherently spiritual about being poor. Even in the Bible in John 2, it says, "Beloved, I wish above all things that thou mayest prosper and be in health even as the soul prospers."

What helped me the most in this matter was to realize that true prosperity actually has a spiritual basis. God does not give us things, but God gives us divine substance, and that substance is just waiting for you to mold it through your thoughts. The spirit within is the mind of abundance, and it is eternally flowing and seeking to appear as abundance on the physical plane. God does not have a problem with you having money; in fact, you could better carry out his purposes with it. Just as long as money does not control you or make you go into greed, wealth is your birthright.

You can have more of life if you have money, and wanting more of life is a good thing. Thinking that the supply is limited is a huge mistake. I happened to know Reverend Ike, who had a church in Harlem. I went once, and it was an old theatre all in gold. The gold organ rose up as if it was coming up from a basement. The black people were dressed to the nines and really happy. He said, "You can go to the ocean with a teaspoon or a bucket, and the ocean does not care." That really made me understand the abundance of the universe.

A man named Wallace Wattles helped me the most. You can look up his teachings right on the Internet. You can download his book, *The Science of Getting Rich*, for free. He has shared it for all. He says there is a science to getting rich. He says the universe desires you to have everything you want to have. He says that the visible supply out there is practically inexhaustible, but the invisible supply is really inexhaustible. He gets you to focus on that divine substance, which is the invisible supply. That formless stuff is alive with creative energy and intelligence; it is always impelled toward more life. In summary, you need to know three things he says.

1. You need to believe that there is one intelligent substance from which all things proceed.
2. You need to believe that this substance gives you everything you desire.
3. You need to relate yourself to that substance in a harmonious way.

The way you relate to it is by deep, profound gratitude. Give thanks continually. Include all things in your gratitude. Gratitude is a surefire way to raise your frequency. The mental attitude of gratitude draws the mind into closer touch with the Source. The law of gratitude must be observed.

When you focus your mind on getting money, you are focusing on the wrong thing and actually shutting off the supply. You are focusing on the effect, not the cause. Money is not your supply. God is. When you forget the cause, the effect starts to diminish.

Remember, the real purpose of money is to serve the world better. My guru Babaji always says that "work is worship" and "idleness is death." When you get up and say, "Oh, Divine Mother, how can I serve you today," everything changes. You will not only enjoy your work, you will be more successful because of that. Love what you are doing or change your job and do something you love. Consider that everyone that you know and everyone that you meet each day is your ministry. Attempting to get money without a service is a violation of the law.

Money, however, will only make you more of what you are. If you are unhappy and you get a lot of money, you might feel more unhappy and suppress it with the money. But eventually, the unhappiness will surface and sabotage things because money is energy and it adds to what you already feel. Anger, fear, and guilt prevent your channel from receiving greater supply, and those things don't automatically go away just by having money. They could increase.

Very successful people think differently. They know they create their own life with their thoughts. They think big. They focus on opportunities. They act in spite of fear. They are bigger than their problems. They are excellent receivers. They spend on things that will improve themselves. They know they are unlimited forever. They know that they are one with everything, not separate. If you think money is out there, then you are separate from it. You are one with the universal energy.

So then if you notice thoughts of poverty, snap out of it! Today you can begin a new life. Start tithing 10 percent and see what happens. You are as prosperous as you decide to be!

As far as your relationship goes, you both need to be clear on the above. It won't work very well if one of you has a prosperity consciousness and the other has a poverty consciousness. Markus and I both came from middle-class families in the Midwest where money was scarce and religion dominated. For that reason, we work on abundance prayers every morning as part of our spiritual practice.

We need to reprogram our minds and erase all of the subconscious conditioning around wealth and money.

Markus on money in the new frequency:

"For Sondra and me, there are certain basic principles that we practice in regard to money that keep it simple and direct, free of conflict. This is our twelve-step plan around money:

1. We agree to have money serve us and our family, friends, and students; we do not serve money.
2. We agree to have gratitude for everything, especially money in whatever amount.
3. We agree to pay all of our bills on time.
4. We agree to be generous and give away money to what we find spiritually uplifting.
5. We agree to spend money wisely and not to waste it.
6. We agree to love what we do that earns money and not to do what we do just to earn money.
7. We agree that credit cards have to be paid off every month so no interest charges are incurred.
8. We agree that we will always live within our means and not spend beyond our means.
9. We agree that the divine substance is our source of wealth, and it has infinite supply for us to mold and shape to produce money.
10. We agree to always be generous, not stingy nor frivolous with money.
11. We agree to be the masters of money, not the victims of it.
12. We agree to always raise our thoughts of giving and receiving, which will raise our prosperity consciousness around money.

"Both of us were brought up with the work ethic, so we like to be productive. Both of us are inclined to be creative and not work for another, so our lives are creative and have something to give. So the money we earn is always from something we like to do and gives us joy in the doing. Everyone must find a way of earning money that is part of his life action of happiness. To just have a job to survive and earn a wage is a misuse of your life energies. This kind of selling of yourself may get you money, but it can often bring about inner conflict, which will eventually exhaust you and wear you out.

"In matters of our work life, Sondra and I earn our money dedicated to our creative and spiritual service. I began to integrate and harmonize with what Sondra had already started. The action of giving seminars; of offering Liberation Breathing sessions and consultations to clients; of writing; and eventually, of painting fit into our mutual work together. We are aligned in this work because we are clear about the spiritual purpose it has for both of us and that we were put together for a mission of divine service. In Babaji's basic teaching of "truth, love, simplicity, and service to mankind," there is no room for disharmony or wasted action. All our work is dedicated to our ascension to fully realize holiness and liberation now as we help others to do the same.

"Our financial situation is simple. We share all of our income. Once our money is earned, we put it together in one fund. We each have our own bank accounts and credit cards in our own names; however, both of us share access to these accounts. It took a little while to set up joint accounts, but we have total transparency in our finances. We do not own property or an automobile, so it keeps our life simple. We travel most of the time, giving workshops and seminars. When we are home, our living expenses are kept simple as well. We rent an apartment in a neighborhood with all the necessities nearby. We walk to the grocery, to the bank, to Walgreens, to the UPS store, to Starbucks, to the many restaurants in our neighborhood. Simplicity is a great asset. When we need a car for a few days, we rent one. We pay our bills on time and have an accountant who figures out what to pay Uncle Sam. We pay our taxes gladly because we receive the benefits of living in an orderly environment and society. We try to save 20 percent of our income. Beyond this, money ceases to be an issue. We feed ourselves spiritually and stay in integrity around money.

"The larger issue in life though goes beyond money as the substance that keeps our lives sustained and maintained. Money is an essential ingredient to life in this world. Without it, we are lost and dependent on others. We need money to be productive and self-reliant. Yet there is a connection with the Source of our sustenance that is absolutely essential, and we need to have spiritual intimacy with that Source.

"*A Course in Miracles has* the final word to say about what sustains us.

I am sustained by the Love of God

Here is the answer to every problem that will confront you, today and tomorrow and throughout time. In this world, you believe you are sustained by everything but God. Your faith is placed in the most trivial and insane symbols; pills, money, "protective" clothing, influence, prestige, being liked, knowing the right people, and an endless list of forms of nothingness that you endow with magical powers.

All these things are your replacements for the Love of God. All these things are cherished to ensure a body identification. They are songs of praise to the ego. Do not put your faith in the worthless. It will not sustain you.

Only the Love of God will protect you in all circumstances. It will lift you out of every trial, and raise you high above all the perceived dangers of this world into a climate of perfect peace and safety. It will transport you into a state of mind that nothing can threaten, nothing can disturb, and where nothing can intrude upon the eternal calm of the Son of God. (ACIM Workbook Lesson 50)"

18

Sex in the New Frequency of Spiritual Intimacy

All that *A Course in Miracles* would have to say about sex is this: are you in the ego's thought system with it or are you in the Holy Spirit's thought system with it? If you are in the ego's thought system, the experience won't be a high frequency, and it could result in being emotionally or physically painful one way or another. If you are in the Holy Spirit's thought system, then it would be sacred sex and a very high frequency. It would be a sharing of not only erotic and sexual intimacy but also an expression of spiritual intimacy.

So then, one has to handle one's negative thoughts about sex and think in a cosmic way. My friend Astarius, who is all about ascension, says celebrate love everywhere and raise all women up if you are a man, and raise all men up if you are a woman. Only then you are in a cosmic romance with the whole universe. He says to see your lover as a cosmic ambassador receiving your love on behalf of the whole universe; otherwise, everything is stopped up with the cork of limitation. Limitation leads to lack. Give your mate the universal package of love. Make him or her the portal. Let your divine love eternally flow. The *Course* would agree with him.

I think it is obvious that if you want spiritual intimacy in sex you, need to be liberated from negativity, selfishness, anger, fear, parental disapproval, negative church dogma, your personal lie, death urge, and birth trauma—conditions discussed earlier.

Sex is totally different when these issues have been resolved and removed. We were all thrilled to find out how Liberation Breathing®

improved our sex lives. For one thing, you breathe more and deeper, having had breathwork. You know yourself and your subconscious after breathwork, so you don't have to hold yourself back because of fear of what might come up. If something comes up, you can breathe yourself right through it while making love.

Warning: If someone who has had a lot of breathwork has sex with someone who has not ever been rebirthed, the latter could get very activated or charged emotionally. Birth memories could come up just being in the aura of someone who has been frequently rebirthed. Experiencing as much pleasure as you do in sex can also activate fear of punishment. That is why church dogma must be released along with the parental disapproval syndrome. When you experience as much aliveness as you do with sex, the fear of running out of it or dying can be activated. That is why we say the frequency totally changes when you have worked out your unconscious death urge or your repressed guilt around sex from religious conditioning.

Sex is always an opportunity to transcend the ego and merge with God and your partner. God approves of you having sex (despite what they may have told you in church as an attempt to control you and your moral behavior). The body is not separate from the Spirit, but is a part of the Spirit to be celebrated. Sex can be a spiritual ceremony when you are in the Holy Spirit's thought system. Sex is then like a sacrament when you partake in the Holy Spirit. That is why you should breathe a lot during sex, and you will be baptized by the Holy Spirit. Sex is innocent.

One day, the following was sent to me on the Internet. It seemed to originate from Lao Tzu, but I am not sure. "A person's approach to sexuality is a sign of his level of evolution. Unevolved persons practice ordinary sexual intercourse. Placing all emphasis upon the sexual organs, they neglect the body's other organs and systems. For those who aspire to the higher realms of living, there is angelic dual cultivation. Because every portion of the body, mind, and spirit yearns for the integration of yin and yang, angelic intercourse is led by the spirit toward this integration rather than by the sexual organs. Where ordinary intercourse is effortful, angelic cultivation is calm, relaxed, quiet, and natural. Where ordinary intercourse unites sex organs with sex organs, angelic cultivation unites spirit with spirit, mind with mind, and every cell of one body with every cell of the other body. Culminating not in dissolution but in integration, it is an opportunity for a man and woman to mutually transform and uplift each other into the realm of bliss and wholeness."

So make your bedroom very beautiful like a temple with altars. Get the books and computers out. It should not be your office! As Astarias would say, "Be taken by love's surprise in every breath that the universe breathes through you and your lover. Make love on the wings of every breath!"

Markus on sex:

"Many spiritual teachers had taken on a vow to be celibate. But we felt ourselves to be aligned with the innocence of sex, and the joy of coming together in an intimate way that could express this joy. The celibacy from attack thoughts and grievances is the real abstention. Sex in itself is innocent and need not be excluded or denied in order to lead a spiritual life. Because we are both aligned in this area, our lovemaking became very powerful and inspiring to us. I wrote this poem to Sondra to express my joy.

Your Lips Upon My Breath

Your Lips are upon my breath, as the
air from me flows into you, and we mingle
in the life-giving elements of our Love.

My lips, then upon yours touching, are
moistened by the dew of your kisses, in
the morning and evening light of our bed.

Your eyes caress mine and I see you as
a child in the total radiance of your earthly
innocence, bestowed on you by Love alone.

I am happy to be with you forever, anticipating
your lips upon my breath over and over again,
day and night they are upon me ceaselessly.

You are a woman, fully developed in your power,
capable of igniting that same God-given power
in this man of your dreams now incarnate before you!

I surrender to your holy mind, and to your holy body,
and see no difference in the joy both together bring,
as the divine physical rises higher to spirit in Love.

My post is hard as I lay beside your supple sweet skin.
Your touch alone makes my member harder still, and
straight to the garden of your Love would I plant myself.

Your eyes and smiling face turn me into youth,
and I am grateful beyond belief for this new vision into
holy realms of innocence this, your presence, brings.

I run my fingers through your hair and shed a tear of pure joy.
It falls upon your soft and fertile breasts, feeding an all pervasive
Love, dissolving all my sorrow with their milk of forgiveness.

Your kisses run happily over hills and dales of my body.
I am the terrain of your journey in the realms of sexual bliss.
I am the innocence found inside yourself and also inside me.

Your lips are upon my breath. I cannot live without them now.
Our inhales are one; our exhales expelling the very nature of
Divinity, which heals and makes our life together whole.

I sing praises to your lips. They are the harbinger of happiness
that is perfect, that which proceeds out of the Mouth of God.
Inside us both, we co mingle with the elements of saints.

We go forth to a tired world, holding the fire of our holy union out
to light the way. Through our Love, may we heal and be healed.
Your lips are upon my breath, and I am YOUR SERVANT forever
more.

"Lovemaking is a service of spiritual intimacy you provide to your partner. It is a giving, not a getting. What does it mean to serve another? Can a person serve without being subservient? Service liberates people from their self-centeredness and introduces them to a finer energy in life that always has something of its own to give. I had found a new respect for the woman that was in my life. It was natural for me to relate to her in terms of service. I did not feel under her "ceiling," but just the opposite. I had a new freedom to express my real nature, my talents, and my passions. Our relationship became the vessel for total communication, total freedom, total trust and power not excluding the sexual aspects.

"As our lovemaking became more intensified and refined, I began to be more open in my poetic expressions. Sexual innocence and beauty entered the spiritual intimacy of songs. We played wonderful music during sex. We were honest with each other about what we liked and did not hold anything back. Both of us wanted to serve the other's joy by giving and receiving our passion. I wrote this poem in the aftermath of a lovely summer evening.

Summer Love

The joy in me arises anticipating your body next to mine,
as lovers intertwined in those ecstatic moments
given to the union of our souls as well.

Our apartment is quiet in the midsummer calm of early night,
upon those cushions so plush and sweet, your form relaxed
and receptive to my touch, and to my Love.

We kiss as our mouths explore the taste of moistened lips,
and we enter each other's oracle of soothing breath, the warm
inhale and exhale of joy's intoxication.

I explore the inner folds of your velvet garment,
and slowly slide my attention to your darkened zones
of ever giving female gifts.

Your nipples arouse me as I kiss them to erection
and lick the ringlets of soft life givers until your cooing
sounds draw me to the home of my most ecstatic devotions.

Now, in the garden of lower regions the flower of your portal
opens its petals to receive my affections. The sweetened taste
of your climax feeds my satisfaction.

Slowly my tongue of angels brings you to heightened cries
of delight as you burst into complete and perfect happiness,
as I become the servant of your erotic fantasy.

And at your side I stand to give you my food of holy nectar.
My saline gift from the milky sea of my love shoots softly
to feed you my adoration in this lounge of summer love."

19

The Formula for Happiness

Each person in a pair is responsible for his or her happiness. But wouldn't it be nice to have an actual formula for happiness?

It has been said that joy is the highest expression of God that there is. If we wish for joy in our lives, we must remember that we were made in the image of God and we are godlike. Loving God is pure joy! I wrote about pure joy in my book with that title. Babaji himself gave us a real formula for happiness and here it is

- truth,
- love,
- simplicity,
- service to mankind.

Then he gave us the mantra Om Namaha Shivai and Liberation Breathing/breathwork to clear ourselves.

He said our highest duty is service to mankind. He repeatedly said, and I repeat, "Work is worship and idleness is death." Work dedicated to God is called karma yoga. You may already be in a service-orientated career. If you are not, you can either change careers or figure out how to be of more service within your current career. See your work as the form of worship it is. All work can be considered service if you have the right attitude. Your line of service could be cultural, political, scientific, religious, philosophical, psychological, financial, or whatever. If you are unclear what it should be, start by offering up your willingness for the divine plan of your life to manifest.

There are so many ways to be of service outside of one's career. Bill Clinton wrote a fabulous book on the subject called *Giving*. There are many groups listed that you can choose to give to.

Are you willing to be part of the new group of world servers? Alice Bailey asked that precise question in her book *Serving Humanity*. She said it is our task to aid the work of the spiritual hierarchy as it is responsible for the evolution of the planet. The masters are always searching for those who are sensitive to the plan, those who have no selfish motives, those who desire nothing but to serve. The masters are busy preparing those souls for constructive work and, eventually, for initiation. Her very profound book explains how the system works and how souls earn the right for higher initiation based on levels of service.

Imagine the person who is deluded by the idea that there is no other way but his way or the person who is oriented by the expression of his personality. Imagine the person who is run by sheer ambition, addicted to competition, the glamour of personal ego power, and the accumulations of material things. Imagine the person who is responding merely to physical needs and the satisfaction of desires, or the person who is jealous of others. Imagine the person who is largely self-centered. Finally, imagine the risk this kind of person runs of making huge mistakes and accruing karma. It is the road to unhappiness.

Now imagine a person who has achieved peace and quiescence, whose very brain cells are falling into the larger divine rhythm. Imagine the person who has love for all beings irrespective of who they may be, the person who is determined to do what is best for all of humanity. Imagine the person who has right thinking, decent behavior, and constant kindness.

Imagine the person who works on achieving constant inner spiritual growth, whose character is essentially humility, who is constantly working to purify himself and then making a difference for humanity. It is the road to happiness.

Now imagine a couple where both embody the latter. Can you see how the latter group deserves to live in the aura of the masters and receive their higher initiations? Serving humanity points out that as your love for humanity increases and your interest in yourself decreases, so you will move toward the center of light and love where the masters stand.

The greatest respect is due Alice Bailey (1880–1949), who described the majority of her work telepathically to be dictated by the Tibetan master Djwhal Khul. In *Serving Humanity*, they say, "Sooner or later a soul arrives at the realization of the futility of constant material ambition. This could take eons of lifetimes. But when the soul arrives at this point, a high state of integration is marked and there is a huge shift of consciousness. The soul then longs to function as part of the greater whole."

The authors point out that if you are not yet at that point, you should "stand on the side of those who are silently and steadily building a new order." Lend your support. If you cannot yourself teach or write, give of your thoughts and your money so that others can.

Markus's experience of service:

"Service is a profound practice that manifests in many different ways, but the root of it begins with a discovery in yourself that you have something to give the world. It could be your time, your skills, your caring, or just the simple peace and quietude you discover within yourself that you give. Service has no bounds, and it takes the core of your being home to the very nature of its divinity itself, which always gives and never takes. Tara Singh spoke to us about the joy of service and inspired us to serve at Mother Teresa Missions for a period of time. The lessons were profound and life changing.

"On one cool fall morning, I got up at 4:00 a.m. and drove myself up from Philadelphia to Brooklyn, New York, to the Mother Teresa Mission I had seen on a video about Mother Teresa's life. I had found the telephone number from information and called the sisters there to offer my services. They said come on Saturday and arrive at 7:00 a.m. So I set out in the dark and arrived on time, just past Yankee Stadium. Not quite knowing what to expect in a neighborhood that was low income and marginal, I parked my car, looked over my shoulder a bit, and knocked on their door. A short and smiling lady from India dressed in an all-white sari with a triple stripe of blue on the fabric's edge greeted me, and without much ado, she showed me to the kitchen. This was a shelter for the homeless, and every day, the sisters prepared a breakfast meal for anyone who came off of the street. They put me to work setting the tables. When the people arrived, I served the food to them. After the meal, I helped clean up the dishes and mop the floor.

"The next week, I had another project in mind for them. Because I noticed their kitchen faucet was old and leaking, I purchased a new one and took my tools and plumbing parts with me on the next visit. After the soup kitchen duties were complete, I surprised the sisters by installing the new faucet. They were delighted, and I felt like this job was more satisfying than any of the many bathrooms and kitchens I had built for my very affluent clients. The sisters asked me, 'Oh, where are you from?' When I said Philadelphia, they exclaimed, 'Why don't you go to our mission in Norristown, just outside of Philadelphia?' There was a mission right in my backyard, and I didn't even know it.

"The next week, I began going there, and for over three years, I went once a week to assist in the soup kitchen, perform various building projects, and even housed a homeless man for a few weeks in the winter. I am not a do-gooder by nature, but I discovered the one who I really served was the still and silent being inside of myself. At first I had to overcome the usual expectations that the poor should be grateful for my labors. Wrong. They were quite the opposite, very rude and crude, angry and ungrateful; that is why they were homeless and poor. But so what? I was there to discover I had something in myself to give. The sisters spoke of service as a privilege. They dedicated all their actions to Jesus and to the action of giving to Him through the distressing disguise of the poor. They lived a life of nonreaction.

"Service is a very high state of being. It is free of reactions, and it is always looking to meet the needs of what is at hand. It is a very dynamic and productive state, which starts with what it has, and extends inner goodness through giving. My life was transformed by these three years spent in the Missionaries of Charity. I owe a great debt of gratitude to Tara Singh for inspiring me and countless others with the joy of service. He was a man whose every action was dedicated to giving something of the spirit to humanity. He walked in his youth with the likes of Gandhi and Nehru, the liberators of India who demonstrated nonviolence. Service was something in his very blood."

The Highest Potential—The Immortal Couple in the New Frequency

Since life is the highest force in the universe, what if you and your mate (who can be your ascension buddy helping you to go to a higher frequency) were able to take in more and more life every year by doing your spiritual practices and letting go of ego? What is the highest potential for a human being anyway? What if you could rejuvenate the physical body and live as long as you chose (while improving your body) in order to do a spiritual mission? Becoming physically immortal is a choice that can be made. One makes a conscious decision to remain on earth and help humanity. There would have to be a thought transformation leading to the achievement of cell regeneration. We are talking about a transfigured body.

You die because you believe you must. You are hypnotized by the thought: death is inevitable. You were once pure spirit that existed on a higher dimension where there was no aging or death. You can return to this dimension if you stay on the ascension path. The human body is ultimately an energy system. If you master the body as light, you can learn to dematerialize and rematerialize!

The difference between a mortal an immortal is what they think about. The body is totally obedient to the thoughts in your mind. Your body can be a self-regenerating battery always capable of being recharged.

Jesus said in John 8:51, "I tell you this truth. Whoever holds fast to my teachings shall never enter the grave."

However, you would have to give up your addiction to the unconscious death urge. What is that? It is a conglomerate in the subconscious that includes the following:

- The thought that death is inevitable
- The thought that you are separate from God
- Your most negative thought about yourself
- All antilife thoughts
- Past-life memories of dying
- Family traditions
- False religious theology
- The belief in sin
- Guilt (the voice of the ego telling you that you are bad and deserve to die)
- Secret wish to die because you hate your life
- Anger and non-forgiveness

What if you breathed all that out? What if you and your ascension buddy went for the ultimate initiation? What would be the advantages? The obvious ones would be these:

- Increased health
- Increased energy
- Increased creativity
- Enhanced quality of life
- Increased potential for regeneration
- More fun
- More joy
- Increased intelligence
- Feeling better than you ever felt before

A yogi once taught me a quick definition of physical immortality by saying, "Spirit is that which cannot be destroyed. Mind is condensed spirit. Body is condensed mind. Therefore, body is utmost spirit." Read that again until you get it.

If you get that completely, physical immortality makes sense. But if you think you are separate from the Spirit, it won't make any sense at all. Physical immortality is the integration of spirit, mind, and body. You have to master the philosophy of it, the psychology of it, and the physiology of it.

In a nutshell, the philosophy of it is that we are already pure spirit. The psychology of it is that you have to unravel your personal death urge. The physiology of it is that you have to be aware of your body as an energy system.

We are talking about living fully, that is, not letting anything come between you and your spirituality. Life without death is pure life. It is like being in a constant rebirth. You get new air. It is a progressive movement into divine truth, and it comes in stages

The ability to lead a long life comes when the body is not forced to do what it does not want. You must clear out of yourself everything that holds you to a reality you do not like.

Imagine your biology ascending.

If you are serious, an immortal friend of mine suggests that you take an actual vow. A vow is alive and is a dimension beyond an affirmation. It involves calling in a witness. You go to a power spot, set up an altar, and you say something like this, "I dedicate my true will to the attainment of physical immortality and the goal of ascension." Then you state ten reasons why it is great to be alive.

Do you still think this is preposterous? Perhaps if you read on, you will open to it more. I found an article in India called "The Last Initiation" by Haridas Chaudhuri, a Bengali integral philosopher. It is the best summary I have found on the subject.

Finally, the concept of immortality implies a harmonization of the entire personality and transformation of the physical organism as an effective channel of expression of higher values. This may be called material immortality.

There are some mystics and spiritual seekers who strengthen and purify their bodies just enough to be able to experience the thrilling touch of the divine. They use the body as a ladder by climbing to the pure spiritual level, the domain of immortality is to be reached. On attaining that level, the body is felt as a burden, as a prison house, as a string of chains that holds one in bondage. Dissociation from this last burden of the body is considered a sine qua non for total liberation. Continued association with the body is believed to be the result of the residual trace of ignorance. When the residual trace of ignorance is gone, the spirit is set free from the shackles of the body.

The above view is based on a subtle misconception about the purpose of life and the significance of the body. The body is not only a ladder that leads to the realm of immortality but also an excellent instrument for expressing the glory of immortality in life and society. It is capable of being thoroughly penetrated by the light of the Spirit. It is capable of being transformed into what has been called the diamond body. As a result of such transformation, the body does not appear any more to be a burden upon the liberated self. It shines as the spirit made flesh! It functions as a very effective instrument for creative actions and realization of higher values in the world. It is purged of all inner tension and conflict. It is liberated from the anxiety of repressed wishes. It is also liberated from the dangerous grip of the death impulse born of self-repression. Mystics who look upon the body as a burden suffer from the anxiety of self-repression and the allurement of the death wish.

Material immortality means decisive victory over both of these demons. It conquers the latent death instinct in man and fortifies the will to live as long as necessary as a channel of expression of the divine. It also liquidates all forms of self-suppression and self-torture and self-mutilation. As a result, the total being of an individual becomes strong and steady, whole and healthy. There is a free flow of psychic energy. It is increasingly channeled into ways of meaningful expression. Under the guidance of the indwelling light of the Eternal, it produces increasing manifestations of the spirit in matter.

What all this does for a relationship is simply incredible. The relationship takes on a whole new vibration of sheer vitality. The sacredness increases also because life is God, and so more life equals more holiness. Spiritual intimacy is extended to include your own relationship to your bodies, which Jesus say is neutral—"The body is a wholly neutral thing" (Lesson 284). So why are we attacking it with illness?

When two immortals are together, there is a sense of wellbeing that pervades the underlying structure of the relationship. They have mastered the art of spiritual intimacy. (I have seen so many relationships where each person is constantly dealing with the suppression of fear, such as when their partner is going to leave them or die.) So instead of getting old and dying together, imagine the opposite! Why not strive for this expression of the divine?

21

How Sondra Used the Cosmic Dating Service to Find Her Man

When I felt ready to have a relationship, I decided I did not want any ordinary relationship. I definitely did not want an unholy relationship. I wanted an extraordinary holy relationship and nothing less. Just one characteristic of that I figured was deep ease. So I thought I had better achieve that in myself first. I meditated on that for an entire year to prepare myself. That was the beginning.

Then I told my master, Babaji, I wanted a cosmic tie, and he could choose my mate. After all, only he would know the karma of any man and the ability to handle the future, and he would know who on earth could handle my lifestyle as a public figure. Not easy! It had to be someone very spiritual and very unique.

On the second year, I began to bring him nearer to me by a means that made my roommates laugh. I bought him (whoever it was) several presents and wrapped them. This was fun and quite a riot since I did not know who I was shopping for. I bought a Brooks Brothers shirt, sandalwood cologne (outstanding!), a wallet, and a white gold ring.

So I had to guess at the size, and since it was expensive, that was a risk for sure. I wrapped these presents and put them under the stairwell.

I was not in a hurry because I knew he would come when I was ready, so I kept on praying to be ready. However, the third year, I got really serious about this. I started doing a mantra every day: "*Sat patim dehi parameshwara.*" You must speak it correctly like this,

"Saht Pah-teem Day-Hee PahRahm EshwarRah" and repeat it 108 times daily on the mala beads. This was enjoyable, and the meaning is this: "I want a man who will honor me and respect my power, who will use my energy honestly and unselfishly without any anger or resentment."

The final thing I did was write him letters as if he was already here. I would start the letters with "Dear Beloved," and I would share all my feelings and so on. This made it quite real. Also I did the affirmation, "I am so happy and grateful that the perfect man for me is here now." You really have to make it real in present time.

I have to admit that I thought I would be meeting some international figure. I never ever dreamed he would come to me in Philadelphia! Markus had been completing a divorce and somehow he got a flyer in the mail that I was doing a seminar in Philadelphia. He decided to come to honor me and give me gratitude for all I had led him to spiritually. I did not even recognize him because I had known him and his wife twenty years ago and he was a Sikh then and totally different. I had lost track of him for twenty years!

The day after the seminar, he came to me for a consultation. I blurted out, "What are you doing here? I mean how could I consult you? You seem so clear!" He told me he had come only to express gratitude, and he gave me a hefty tithe. I then asked him if I could see his art. I did not even get at the time this could be the one, but Babaji took over. Two of Babaji's devotees were there in Philadelphia, Diana from London and Shanti from Paris. They did kind of an intervention on me, and they both said, "Don't you get it? This is the one!" They were so insistent that I started to wake up to the possibility. Markus had given me his journal by chance, and I started reading it. It was so deep. I was shocked!

Here was a man who was a rebirther as I was, *A Course in Miracles* teacher as I was, a writer as I was, a student of Hawaiian Ho'oponopono as I was, and a Babaji devotee, a Divine Mother devotee as I was. Was he, could he be my twin flame in actuality?

I called him and said I needed a new Ho'oponopono(Hawaiian prayer book) as mine was all beat up. He gave me the number of the woman who could help me with that. I e-mailed her, and she said to come over. I called Markus and asked him if he could drive me there, and he said, "Certainly." When I got in his car, I had the shock of my life. He had a huge picture of my kahuna teacher between him and me, and I had never even seen that amazing picture. How many men would even know Morrnah Simeona, let alone have a picture of her? That was a huge breakthrough, and I really opened my heart. He took my assistant and me to dinner after that visit, and I kept saying to myself, "He is so deep." After the dinner, as we walked across the plaza, I put my arm through his and he liked that.

When we got back to the Philadelphia Rebirthing Center, the buzz was that we were already an item. We did not get it totally, but the following week, I was in Asheville, North Carolina, for the first time, and Valentine's Day was coming up. So I called Markus and asked him if he wanted to come down and spend Valentine's Day with me. The rest is history. It was so easy and wonderful.

Later when he came to California, the shirt fit perfectly, he loved the cologne (sandalwood from the Art of Shaving)and even the ring was a perfect fit, believe it or not!

Markus proposed to me in Nashville. We were married in Babaji's ashram a year later. Then we moved to Nashville where we fell in love. We took a honeymoon to Thailand at a spiritual retreat. When we returned to Nashville, we found that our new apartment had been totally decorated, all our things were unpacked, and the clothes were hung. The best part was this, the spiritual art was hung. The place was decorated better than I could have decorated it!.

It was all *done* when we moved in.

22

How My Husband Inspires Me to Change Bad Habits

I have a bad habit of leaving the lights on. Sometimes I am rushing around and go out of my body about it. My husband started out by asking me if I was aware of this pattern. I wasn't. I thanked him for pointing it out. But somehow that was still not enough to have me change. Then he would come out and say, "Could I ask you to turn the lights out?" He would say it so sweetly that I took notice, and I wanted to please him and do this correctly. In fact, the nicer he was, the more I wanted to do it. But then I had some setbacks. Markus would come out and say it this way, "What is it about me that I cannot seem to create you shutting out the lights?" At that point, I felt humbled, and I saw how hard he was trying not to criticize me but at the same time not stuffing in his feelings. He spoke to me so lovingly about it that I really, really, really made the effort. He never got fed up with me. In fact, a few times, he would just go shut the lights out himself. Once he even put up sticky notes to remind me. This would really get to me. He finally just loved me through this pattern all the way. It can be done, and it is a wonderful exercise. I am still perfecting this.

When it came to his issue, I found myself trying to do the same. He never gets angry at me, ever, but he does get irritated at times about money issues. This, I know has to do with his birth as, when he came into the world, his father was ill with hepatitis and out of work. There was a real money issue from the beginning. So when he goes into that pattern, I try to say to him lovingly, "The only time I ever see you get irritated is around money. Do you want a Liberartion Breathing session?" Then we create time to work on it with the breathing. I have had to be as patient with him as he was with me. I finally said, "How could I support you getting more relaxed around the subject of money?" We finally put it all in our morning prayers. So far, we are both making strides although it has taken some time to give up these addictions. Patience is needed. Love is needed. Discussion is needed. I don't feel either of us should stuff it or forget it. I believe we need to help each other with these levels of unconsciousness. I know this for sure: anger would not work for me or for him. I need to stay in my body and become totally aware of my surroundings. He needs to relax on the subject of money. We both know this; we both want this. It is taking time.

I know how hard it can be to break habits. When I am in England or Down Under, I invariably try to get in the wrong side of the car even though I know the passenger's seat is the opposite to that in the US. But it is such a habit that I make the mistake several times before I get it right.

If the issue is huge, the temptation is to be more judging. That is a mistake. One wonderful thing my husband Markus has taught me is this, for bigger issues he says it is "our problem" and he naturally assumes we have created it together since we are one. This is the way of Ho'oponopono. If there is a problem in the family, everyone has to take responsibility for having created this problem together. Quite early on in our relationship I manifested a skin condition. I felt very guilty about this. It was helpful to know the cause, which I learned from a medical intuitive. I was processing five generations back, I was told. But Markus always said, "We have created this, and we have to heal it together." This helped me so much not to feel guilty, which would have only blocked the healing more. When he talked about it as our problem, I felt so supported, and it worked!

You know what they say, "You are the one you live with!"

What always helps me is our number 1 agreement: to have a conflict-free relationship. Since we have both committed to that, it takes top priority. I remember a potential upset we almost had at the airport when they started charging for every bag. It was quite a shock to Markus the first time we traveled together because I pack a lot so that I feel at home on the road. It is important to me. When

Markus heard the checked luggage total, he was not happy. But then he remembered our agreement—no conflict—and he wanted to make me happy, so he dropped it.

What really works for me is remembering to treat my mate the same as I would an honored guest. We have tried to train ourselves to do just that. When we don't do that, it does not work so well. When we do that, things are very, very smooth. My husband deserves that, and why shouldn't he have that kind of treatment since I love him even more than an honored guest? To me, it is all about politeness and tone of voice. It is all about having no anger. I cannot say that enough.

What I Love About My Husband

He is more in love with God/Jesus/Babaji/*A Course in Miracles* than anything else. This is his love of life.

He loves me with that same love, coming from the Spirit first.

He is extremely kind and treats me like an honored guest at home and elsewhere.

He can be with me 24/7 day in and day out, and it is never boring or trying.

He takes responsibility for all his results and knows he creates them himself and never blames me or others.

He makes sure we do our spiritual practices every day and, recently, every night.

He often has the highest thought on any issue.

He is sensitive and feeling his feelings, often crying at the beauty of things.

He is almost never angry, and on the rare occasions where he is irritated, he is willing to get a Liberation Breathing session right away.

He often tells me, "Let's not make it a problem."

He helps me with everything.

He is very intuitive, having worked on himself spiritually for years.

He takes on any problem I have as *our* problem together, making me feel very supported.

He is totally willing to recognize his mistakes, admit them, and do something about them.

He is very patient with my weak points and bad habits (like leaving lights on), pointing them out to me over and over in a kind way that inspires me.

He is open to anything I want to communicate and is not judging.

He can often explain to me the deeper meaning of *A Course in Miracles* when I do not understand it.

He is a very good breathworker, finding the exact right thing to say to clients (and to me) along with the perfect affirmations.

He writes very beautiful poetry, which makes one feel exalted.

He can paint very beautiful paintings, which are spiritual in nature.

He is very easy to be with—no garbage, baggage, or negativity in my space.

He has a way with words when he teaches that I find very enjoyable to listen to.

He inspires my girlfriends to want a man like him, and hopefully, they say, he has a brother who is available. Unfortunately, he has no brothers.

Letting the Maha Avatar Guide
Your Relationship

I have mentioned that Babaji is our master. He helped us find each other and also helps us so much in the guidance of our relationship and our whole life. In case you are interested in this blessing, let me explain who Babaji is.

Babaji, also named Sri Sri 1008 Bhagwan Heerakhan Wale Baba is an immortal maha avatar and yogi master. (Avatar means descent of the divine into matter. He materialized his body and was not born of a woman.) Babaji is an emanation of divine light who, out of compassion, manifested in human form on earth to urge humanity to progress on the path of truth, simplicity, love, and service to mankind. He is the power of the eternal father, mother, and divine child. He can assume any form he wishes and can change that form at any time. He is known as the historical Sada Shiva in Hindu religious literature. However, he is actually beyond all religion. In fulfillment of ancient scriptural and prophetic predictions, he materialized a youthful body in 1970 in a cave near the village of Hairakhan in the foothills of the Himalayas. There are stories of Indian people who witnessed this. Yogananda wrote about him in *Autobiography of a Yogi*.

After he appeared, he climbed the sacred Mount Kailash and sat there for forty-five days without eating, drinking, or sleeping. He stayed in meditation because, if he opened his eyes, people would faint. He was so much pure spirit that they could not handle it at first.

Babaji was accessible in India in his body for fourteen years on his last visit. His visit from 1970 to 1984 was his most recent materialization, yet he has not really left. He does not come and go. He was and is omnipresent. His form is limitless and beyond the scope of time. He is the essence of all religions and transcends every belief. He teaches through vibrations and direct experience in a way that words cannot express.

To try to explain him on paper seems inadequate. To experience him answers all questions. I was fortunate to meet him in the physical body several times. The guru he left in charge named Muniraj, who was called the "King of Silence" and was one of the purest beings on earth, Babaji said. Muniraj told us Babaji was back in a body. We don't know where. But surely he is meditating somewhere in the Himalayas. I predict he will come back to the ashram in five years. I don't really know though.

Babaji is as available for you and for all as he is for us. His healing presence is omnipresent in the whole universe, and you may have miracles in your life with him as we have. He says, "My love is available. You can take it or not." I say, "Why not?"

Each person's relationship with him is unique. He will begin to enter your life and relationship if you ask him to. Introducing you to him is the highest blessing we could offer you besides *A Course in*

Miracles. Jesus, in His travels and studies in India, visited Babaji in Benares. It was there that Babaji shaved Jesus's head and blessed Him before Jesus started his ministry.

We have written a whole book on Babaji called *Babaji: My Miraculous Meetings with a Maha Avatar*, which we know you will also enjoy.

The Gospel of St Thomas says, "If you see him who has not been born of a woman, throw your face to the ground and worship him as he is your Father."

Epilogue

Along time ago, I read a book by Robert Roskind called *In the Spirit of Business*. He mentioned three ways people look at the universe. I went through the first two myself before getting on the path of enlightenment. It was such a relief to get to the third view, which I know to be the truth. This book is based on that truth. If you really take it in, you will start to understand yourself as you truly are and only this will lead to peace.

There is one view of the universe where there is no creator, and it is a random universe and planet. This is the pattern in which people with that belief feel they are lucky or unlucky to encounter situations and people in their lives. This can lead to feeling helpless and being out of control. The person feels "life just happens to me." It is really victim consciousness. All that they strive to accomplish can be suddenly destroyed. Lives have no purpose, and safety is uncertain.

There is another view, a created universe, but it is punitive and indifferent. A punitive God rules the universe. This is most commonly being taught in most traditional religions. Painful relationships and situations are then "proof" of our sin. We then deserve the punishment we get in our lives, eventually ending in disease and death. We believe others have sinned against us. God allows us to suffer. There is still a lot of fear in this model. If there is a heaven, it exits in the afterlife, and we may or may not end up there. If we are good and endure our suffering here, maybe we will get our rewards on the other side. If we are bad, then well, more suffering on the other side. Or out of the pain we feel inflicted on us, we rebel and renounce God altogether and go for the gusto ourselves and make things happen according to our plan.

There is another view of the universe, a created universe with a totally benevolent creator and planet. It places us as the cocreator of our universe. We are the cause, not the effect, of our lives and relationships. The people in our lives are there to teach us love. We have called each person and situation into our life, and we must say, "What is the lesson?" This view offers us comfort and safety. Nothing is an accident or a punishment. All things are lessons and opportunities. In this model, the planet is a huge schoolroom. We have free will to choose what we want to learn. But the curriculum is this, to learn unconditional love in all circumstances. Self-discovery of who we really are (Love) is our goal. We all enter at different grades depending on our past lives. The differences in spiritual awakening is why we see some people really loving and others not.

This book is obviously based on the latter view, and if you allow yourself to see life this way, you will experience a whole new world—the forgiven world. We share with everyone the mission of discovering our true nature. We share through having spiritual intimacy in the new frequency for relationships.

If we see the universe as only benevolent and loving and offering us gifts in the forms of lessons, fear is no longer appropriate but needs to be recognized and released. We can relax and enjoy the process. When we accept as our purpose being here to learn and teach love and remove the blocks to love, it changes our outlook. We begin to love looking at ourselves and processing ourselves; then introspection and inner correction becomes a joy. Where there is no introspection, people get *stuck*. When we see the universe as it really is, i.e., benevolent, then we can have the guidance and support we need to make our relationships work.

Once you see the universe correctly and clear yourself, there is no reason you cannot create anything you want in life and relationships. People think relationships are hard. They don't have to be. They can be very wonderful and exciting the rest of your life. But the secret that I have found is the idea of Spiritual Intimacy. After teaching thousands of students of all ages, and giving breathwork to thousands of people of all ages, and counseling people of all ages, I can honestly say this is what people are looking for—spiritual intimacy. Ask yourself. Isn't this what you are looking for?

Do you know what Oprah Winfrey said was the main thing she learned after twenty-five years of doing her television show? The answer was, "People just want to be heard." I would agree, and don't ever forget that. You know what I have learned after thirty-five plus years of doing this work? People want spiritual intimacy in their relationships. And I am not talking about going to church and learning religious dogma. I am talking about sharing your spiritual growth with your mate and being on a spiritual path with your mate that is real, alive, and moving toward more and more life. And it is all about communication, communication, communication that can lead to communion with the sacred.

Our prayer is that this book becomes your playbook to practicing and exploring and discovering more spiritual intimacy in your life. It has been an act of spiritual intimacy for us while writing it. We send you all our blessings for spiritual intimacy to be your new way of life in a holy relationship for you!

Love,
Sondra and Markus

Resources

Certified Liberation Breathing® Facilitators

Sondra Ray /– author, teacher, rebirther, creator of the Loving Relationships Training™, Co-founder of Liberation Breathing®
Facebook: https://www.facebook.com/sondra.ray.90
Facebook Fan Page: https://www.facebook.com/LiberationBreathing
Twitter: https://twitter.com/SondraRay1008
YouTube: https://www.youtube.com/SondraRay
Website: https://www.sondraray.com/
Blog: http://www.liberationbreathing.blogspot.com

Markus Ray /– poet, author, artist, rebirther, presenter of *A Course in Miracles*, co-founder of Liberation Breathing®,
Facebook: https://www.facebook.com/markus.ray.169
Facebook Fan Page: https://www.facebook.com/LiberationBreathing
Twitter: https://twitter.com/MarkusRay1008
Website: http://www.markusray.com/
Website: http://www.miraclesarepresent.com/
Art Look Blog: https://markusray.wordpress.com/

3000 Vanderbilt Place, Apt. #118
Nashville, Tenessee.N 37212

E-mail: immortalrayproductions@gmail.com

For Certified Liberation Breathing® Facilitators go here:
https://www.sondraray.com/practitioners

Denise Dobbs, Ft. Lauderdale, Florida, USA
Tove Jensen, Copenhagen, Denmark
Taj Chana, London, United Kingdom
Adailton Soares, Belo Horizonte, Brazil
Laura Carrasco Verde, Barquisimeto, Venezuela
Maria Jose Borras, Valencia, Spain
Lia Schultz, Boynton Beach, Florida, USA

Babaji and The Divine Mother Resources:
Haidakhandi Universal Ashram/Crestone. Colorado, USA
www.babajiashram.org

Babaji's Ashram in Haidakhan (India)
E-mail: info@haidakhanbabaji.com
Haidakhandi Samaj (India)
E-mail: Info@HaidakhandiSamaj.org

Planetbabaji
www.planetbabaji.com

Bibliography

Airola, Dr. Paavo. *Are You Confused?* Sherwood, OR: Health Plus Publishers, 1984.

Amitraswarupananda. *Awaken Children.* Castro Valley, CA: MA Center, 1991.

Anonymous. *A Course in Miracles.* Tiburon, CA: Foundation for Inner Peace, 1985.

Bailey, Alice. *Serving Humanity.* New York: Lucas Publishing Co, 1972.

Bragg, Paul. *The Miracle of Fasting.* Santa Barbara, CA: Bragg Health Sciences, 1999.

Clinton, Bill. *Giving: How Each of Us Can Change the World.* New York: Alfred A. Knopf, 2007.

Fortune, Dion. *The Esoteric Philosophy of Love and Marriage.* York Beach, ME: Samuel Weiser, 2000.

Geraghty, Anne. *How to Make Your Relationship Work.* London: Collins & Brown, 2003.

Hawkins, David R. *Power vs. Force: the Hidden Determinants of Human Behavior.* Sedona, AZ: Veritas Publishing, 1995.

Kriyanandai. *How to Spiritualize your Marriage.* Nevada City, CA: Crystal Clarity Publishers, 1992.

Meyers, Anne and Peter. *Being a Christ!: Inner Sensitivity (Intuitional) Training Course.* Lemon Grove, CA: Dawning Publications, 1983.

Price, John Randolph. *Practical Spirituality.* Carlsbad, CA: Hay House, 1996.

Osho. *A New Vision of Women's Liberation.* New Delhi, India: Full Circle Publishing, 2008.

Ray, Sondra and Markus. *A Guaranteed Miracle from Babaji.* Nashville, TN: unpublished, 2009.

Ray, Sondra. *Pele's Wish.* Maui, HI: Inner Ocean Publishing, 2005.

Ray, Sondra. *Rock Your World with the Divine Mother.* Novato, CA: New World Library, 2007.

Ray, Sondra. *The Only Diet There Is.* Berkeley, CA: Celestial Arts, 1981.

Schucmann, Helen. *Song of Prayer: Prayer, Forgiveness and Healing.* Tiburon, CA: Foundation for Inner Peace, 1982.

Singh, Tara. *How to Raise a Child of God.* Los Angeles: Life Action Press, 1987.

Sutphen, Dick. *You Were Born Again to be Together.* New York: Pocket Books, 1987.

Tannen, Deborah. *You Just Don't Understand: Women and Men in Conversation.* New York: Quill, of Harper Collins, 2001.

Woolger, Robert. *Other Lives Other Selves: A Jungian Psychotherapist Discovers Past Lives.* New York: Bantam Books, 1988.

Yogananda, Paramahansa. *Autobiography of a Yogi.* Los Angeles, CA: Self Realization Fellowship, 1998.

Zukav, Gary. *The Seat of the Soul.* New York: Fireside Books, 2001.

About the Authors

Sondra Ray is known the world over as one of the most dynamic spiritual leaders of our day. She is recognized by many as a spiritual teacher, author, lecturer, and healer, with a renowned expertise in the area of relationships, sacred lifestyles, Sacred Quests, and Rebirthing/ Breathwork she now calls Liberation Breathing®.

Sondra graduated with a degree in nursing from the University of Florida in the early 1960's. Inspired by President Kennedy's inauguration speech, she was a pioneer in the first 10 groups of the **Peace Corps**, an experience that gave her the lifelong dedication to world service. After the **Peace Corps** she served her country as a US Air Force nurse, during the Vietnam era, counseling the families of pilots killed in action.*

In the early 1970's Sondra Ray teamed with Leonard Orr who together explored the effects of the "birth trauma" and its detrimental subconscious influence on a person's life. They discovered the powerful use of conscious connected breathing (Rebirthing) to be an effective practice to help people clear these memories of early life trauma very quickly from their mind and body. Sondra went on to write over 20 books on the subjects of Rebirthing, relationships, ideal birth, The Forgiveness Diet©, *A Course in Miracles*, healing and holiness, and the many mental & spiritual imperatives in life…

Author **Marianne Williamson** says of Sondra Ray:

> *"…those who explored the frontiers of universal spiritual consciousness were true pioneers. Their ideas were mind blowing and life altering for an entire generation, for whom such beliefs were startlingly outside the box. One of those pioneers was Sondra Ray…If Sondra writes a new book, I read it. I let go of my left brain and drink her in, imagining her sitting on a chair, explaining to me what to her is so obvious and the rest of us, well, maybe not so much. I have never experienced Sondra as anything other than a beam of light…I have lived enough to be able to say that of all the good fortunes I have had in my life, encountering her has been one of the liveliest. Sondra Ray is more than a woman…The word GODDESS comes to mind…"*

From Marianne Williamson's Foreword in Sondra's book, **Rock Your World with the Divine Mother**.

Ray was launched into international acclaim in the 1970s as one of the pioneers of the Rebirthing Experience. She has trained thousands of people all over the world in this conscious connected breathing process, and is considered one of the foremost experts on how the birth trauma affects one's body, relationships, career and life. As she puts it, "This dynamic breathing process produces extraordinary healing results in all of your relationships—with your mate, with yourself and with Life—very fast. By taking in more Life Force through the breath, limiting thoughts and memories, which are the cause of all problems and disease, come to the surface of the mind so they can be 'breathed out', forgiven and released."

Now Sondra Ray has taken Rebirthing to a new level of effectiveness by invoking the Divine Mother energy into the breathing sessions. One of her recent books, **Rock Your World with the Divine Mother**, emphasizes the importance of a fundamental paradigm shift out of the conventional "patriarchal model" of relationships into a more balanced equality between the Masculine and Feminine polarities. This has also been an influence on her teachings in the Breathwork field. In her latest book, **Liberation Breathing®: The Divine Mother's Gift**, she describes a new expression of Rebirthing in which attention is paid to the underlying Life Force of matter, referred to as the Divine Mother Energy. This Energy has great healing potential as invoked in the *Liberation Breathing®* process.

Often ordained as the "Mother of Rebirthing/Breathwork", Sondra created and teaches various seminars, including her most popular *Loving Relationships Training®*, which has evolved into the *New LRT®*, which will soon be offered as an online interactive course. This training has helped thousands of people get clear on their relationships. It explains common negative family patterns and helps people overcome them through applying practices of *Liberation Breathing®* and affirmations of creative thought. Ray has taken these seminars and practices across the globe to countries such as England, France, Spain, Italy, Germany, Iceland, Ireland, Poland, Sweden, Estonia, Russia, New Zealand, Australia, Singapore, Bali and Japan. She also takes groups to India, Glastonbury, Iceland, Bali and Hawaii for annual pilgrimages. See here for other course offerings: https://www.sondraray.com/seminars-training

Sondra Ray also had the privilege of spending time with the immortal Master, Maha Avatar Haidakhan Babaji, in India on several occasions from 1977-1984, becoming His lifelong student and disciple. For the past 30 years she has led groups to India and introduced thousands to the deep spiritual heritage this country has to offer. Her India Quest is given every Spring, on which she takes people to the Banks of the Ganges, to Haidakhan, to participate in the Spring Navaratri, a nine day spiritual festival dedicated to honoring the Divine Mother—the feminine aspects of the Divine Nature that permeates all Life. Participants are also immersed in the *Liberation Breathing*® process daily during the India Quest, her most powerful offering of the year. Ms. Ray currently travels the world teaching, and has a private healing practice with her husband, Markus Ray. They conduct private sessions in person and over Skype. People who have worked with Sondra Ray & Markus Ray say their teachings, their guidance, their dynamic presence, and the *Liberation Breathing*® process have saved them years of time in getting clear on relationships and what has been blocking their spiritual evolution.

Sondra was one of the first to lecture on and teach *A Course in Miracles*, since the late 1970's. She has said, "*A Course in Miracles* is the most important book written in 2000 years." Together with her husband, Markus, who studied *ACIM* with pre-eminent teacher, Tara Singh** for 17 years, they travel the world speaking on this profound scripture. Tara Singh has described *A Course in Miracles* as *"A Gift for all Mankind"*, destined to be one of the greatest gifts America has contributed to the world of spiritual literature. Sondra & Markus's audio lectures on the valuable principles of ACIM are available at www.SondraRay.com as *Dialogues on A Course in Miracles* and also on their www.MiraclesArePresent.com website.

Applying over 40 years of metaphysical study, Ray has helped thousands of people discover how their negative thought structures, birth trauma, habitual family patterns and unconscious death urge have affected their life. She encourages people to make lasting positive changes through *Liberation Breathing*® to be more free, happy and productive. No matter what Sondra Ray is doing, she is always trying to bring about a higher consciousness. Recently she has written a new book yet to be released on the subject of her spiritual Master *BABAJI: My Meetings With A Real Avatar*, which she envisions will shift the current paradigm in relationships around the world to a new level of consciousness, free from anger and conflict.

Sondra Ray and Markus Ray on their wedding day in India

Markus Ray received his training in the arts, holding an MFA in painting from Tyler School of Art, Temple University in Philadelphia, PA, USA. Also a writer and a poet, he brings spirituality and sensuality together in these mediums of expression. He is the author of a major work, ***Odes To The Divine Mother***, which contains 365 prose poems in praise of the Divine Feminine Energy. Along with the ***Odes*** are his paintings and images of the Divine Mother created around the world in his mission with Sondra Ray. This work will be available in May of 2015 on Amazon. Markus is a presenter of the profound modern psychological/spiritual scripture, ***A Course In Miracles***. He studied ***ACIM*** with his master, Tara Singh, for 17 years, in order to experience its truth directly. His spiritual quest has taken him to India many times with Tara Singh and Sondra Ray, where Muniraj, Babaji's foremost disciple, gave him the name Man Mohan, "The Poet who steals the hearts of the people".

In all of his paintings, writings and lectures, Markus creates a quiet atmosphere of peace and clarity that is an invitation to go deeper into the realms of inner stillness, silence and beauty. He teaches, writes and paints along side of Sondra Ray, and many have been touched by their demonstration of a holy relationship in action. His iconic paintings of the Masters can be viewed on www. MarkusRay.com which he often creates while his twin flame, Sondra Ray, is lecturing in seminars.

Babaji, Jesus and the Divine Mother painted in Italy, Brazil and Spain

Sondra Ray & Markus Ray are brought together by the grace of their Master, Maha Avatar Herakahn Babaji. Babaji Himself said, "Markus is my humbleness. Sondra is my voice. together they are my Love." As ambassadors for Him, their mission is to bring His teaching of "Truth, Simplicity, Love and Service to Mankind" along with the presence of the Divine Mother to the world. They do so through seminars like the *New LRT*®, the healing practice of *Liberation Breathing*®, and the study of *A Course in Miracles*. They are unfolding the plan of Babaji, Jesus and the Divine Mother, which is beyond our wildest dreams! Their relationship is a shining example of what is possible through deep ease and no conflict. They can take you to a higher realm where spiritual intimacy, miracles, and holy relationships can become real in your life. Their various Sacred Quests around the world with *Liberation Breathing*® prepare many to heal their relationships, to receive more profound levels of divine presence in their lives, and awaken more awareness of immortal Love in their hearts. Markus writes this early poem of his relationship with Sondra:

My Immortal Love for You

My Immortal Love for You is beyond the stars.

My Immortal Love for You is never ceasing, but strong from the heart of the Master within us.

My Immortal Love for You is in the quiet of the night which envelops our sleep in sweetness.

My Immortal Love for You fuels my desire to place myself within the inner spaces of your receptive pull.

My Immortal Love for You rests in the cozy safety of refuge amidst all thunderous storms.

My Immortal Love for You makes all its beautiful sounds of music in the cadence of daily speech.

My Immortal Love for You provides all that we need in this world.

My Immortal Love for You has no fear, no matter what our situation may look like.

My Immortal Love for You cannot be extinguished in any way.

My Immortal Love for You is a beacon of light when all other lights have gone out.

My Immortal Love for You is the reason I am here now.

My Immortal Love for You is the source of all my songs.

My Immortal Love for You pervades the molecules of all things seen and unseen.

My Immortal Love for You lifts other souls to the heights of their own immortal being.

My Immortal Love for You is the spark of my internal fires.

My Immortal Love for You warms my whole body in the cold caverns of temporary doubt.

My Immortal Love for You is the first thought in my day and the last thought before my sleep.

My Immortal love for You is the medicine for all my sickness, the balm that heals all of my wounds.

My Immortal Love for You is the well of infinite waters into which your ladle dips to quench your thirst.

My Immortal Love for You is the new beginning that holds out its infinite promise of perfect happiness.

So would I immerse myself in You, the spring that feeds forever this awareness of my Immortal Love for You.

*In her early formative years before her life mission as a Rebirther, teacher and author, Ray earned a B.S. degree in Nursing from the University of Florida College of Nursing, and a Masters Degree in Public Health and Family Sociology from the University of Arizona. She was trained as a Nurse Practitioner in Obstetrics and Gynecology. During her assignment in the Peace Corps she was stationed in Peru, which prepared her for world service. During her service in the US Air Force she was stationed at Luke Air Force Base in Arizona.

**Tara Singh, author, humanitarian, lecturer on *A Course in Miracles* was trained by Mr. J. Krishnamurti for over 30 years to prepare him for 3 years in silence...out of which came the blessing of his meeting with Dr. Helen Schucman, the scribe of *A Course in Miracles*. It was his intense relationship with Dr. Schucman, on a daily basis for over 2 and 1/2 years, that served to ordain Tara Singh as one of the most authentic voices on this modern day scripture available in these times.

Printed in the USA
CPSIA information can be obtained
at www.ICGtesting.com
LVHW040351300823
756589LV00002B/343

9 781681 399317